The
POLITICAL
Spirit

BOOKS BY FAISAL MALICK

POSITIONED TO BLESS

THE DESTINY OF ISLAM IN THE END TIMES

THE POLITICAL SPIRIT

AVAILABLE FROM DESTINY IMAGE PUBLISHERS

The
POLITICAL
Spirit

FAISAL MALICK

DESTINY IMAGE® PUBLISHERS, INC.

P.O. Box 310, Shippensburg, PA 17257-0310

"Speaking to the Purposes of God for this Generation and for the Generations to Come."

This book and all other Destiny Image, Revival Press, Mercy Place, Fresh Bread, Destiny Image Fiction, and Treasure House books are available at Christian bookstores and distributors worldwide.

For a U.S. bookstore nearest you, call 1-800-722-6774.

For more information on foreign distributors, call 717-532-3040.

Reach us on the Internet at www.destinyimage.com.

ISBN 10: 0-7684-2733-9   ISBN 13: 978-0-7684-2733-2

For Worldwide Distribution, Printed in the U.S.A.

1 2 3 4 5 6 7 8 9 10 11 / 13 12 11 10 09 08

DEDICATION

I dedicate this book to the millions who will conquer the political spirit and rise up as leaders in this season to impact and change our world. To the many who have lost battles to this enemy but will win the war. To the end-time Church, that will usher in an era of divine government that will rest upon the shoulders of our soon coming King Jesus Christ.

ENDORSEMENTS

Faisal Malick unmasks the mastermind spirit behind end-time deception. A must read.

Sid Roth
Host, "It's Supernatural!"

The Political Spirit presents Faisal Malick's fresh look at spiritual warfare, the sovereignty of God, and our role and authority as individual Christians and as the Body of Christ. He gives clear and practical help to overcome the schemes satan deploys to keep us from all God has called us to be. When political correctness takes precedence over uprightness before God, the Church is in danger of falling prey to the Political Spirit. In this gripping book Faisal Malick once again verbalizes a fresh revelation from God to His Church. He is urging the Church to be about our Father's business.

Dr. Ronald V. Burgio
President, Elim Fellowship

Many know that I have written both *The Future War of the Church* and *God's Unfolding Battle Plan*. Both of these books describe the times and seasons we are living in and how to maneuver through the major Kingdom war theaters. If I could recommend one other book to go with these two books it would be *The Political Spirit* by Faisal Malick. If we understand what Faisal is communicating, it prevents us from falling into the same snare that Judas fell into. There is a great handshake between the political and religious arenas. Jesus told us to beware of "the leaven of the Pharisees and the leaven of Herod." The Church has become entwined and common with the political system in its operation, resulting in us looking like worldly kingdoms instead of the Kingdom of God. Faisal has written the best explanation of the Herodian Dynasty that I have read. He has related this to militant Islam and how there will be a final battle for power in the days ahead. He is one who has experiential knowledge of this arena. *The Political Spirit* is a must read!

Dr. Chuck D. Pierce
President, Global Spheres, Inc.
President, Glory of Zion International
Harvest Watchman, Global Harvest Ministries

The first time I sat down with Faisal Malick to hear his insights on the political spirit, I was blown away. He made me hunger for more revelation on how to discern its pernicious mine fields. Jesus instructed us to "Beware of the leaven of the Pharisees and of Herod." The leaven of Herod, (the political spirit) needs to be both exposed and overcome. You will be amazed at the revelation you receive as you read through this Spirit-inspired work. Great job, Faisal!

Patricia King
XPmedia.com

CONTENTS

Preface

A Change
of Seasons

Change is afoot. There is a shifting and shaking and an unsettling that is occurring throughout the Church—as well as around the world. God is preparing to reestablish His divine order—His Kingdom on the earth. Many think He has withdrawn His hand from human affairs, but that is not true. He is actively sifting and shifting His people—drawing them into their places to accomplish His preordained purposes. He is preparing His Church, aligning His Body, and empowering His holy people to walk in the authority required to emerge victorious in these last days.

In Ecclesiastes 3:17, Solomon wrote, *"...There is a time for every purpose and for every work."* In other words, there is a proper order—or season—for all things to be done. When Ecclesiastes was translated from Hebrew to Greek, the word used for "time" or "season" here was *kairos*. We are entering such a time now—a *kairos* time—a special season appointed by God for His intervention in human history.

When Ecclesiastes was translated from Hebrew to Greek, the word used for "time" or "season" here was *kairos*.

We are entering such a time now—a kairos time—a special season appointed by God for His intervention in human history.

As this time draws near, God is preparing His Church. Whatever He does in the earth among His people requires a season of preparation. As the master husbandman, God carefully prepares the soil and the seed before it is sown. There are God-given seasons for fallowing the ground, planting, cultivating, pruning, and finally harvesting. Each season requires attentiveness and patience. God is both attentive and patient as He prepares the earth, His Church, and the whole earth to be filled with the knowledge of His glory.

His Church, and the whole earth to be filled with the knowledge of His glory.

However, the Bible tells us that when, *"The sower sows the word....Satan comes immediately and takes away the word that was sown in their hearts"* (Mark 4:14-15). As the Church prepares for the glory of God, satan has a strategy to come in, steal that word, and choke out what God is trying to do before it even sprouts. He has assigned his most successful and powerful agent to upend the coming of God's glory, and we need to be ready to thwart this spirit of deception. This ancient spiritual strategy of the enemy has caused the greatest moves of God in history to fizzle into ineffectiveness and impotence, destroying them from within through power struggles, strife, and hidden agendas. It is a spirit that, up until now, has been largely unknown, as it always hides behind others to do its dirty work. Your eyes are about to be opened to an invisible intelligence that is the strong man of our times. As the Scriptures and history unfold in this book, you will recognize this crafty entity as "the political spirit."

It is time for the façade of corrupt governing systems and religious hypocrisy of our day to be exposed. You will get a behind-the-scenes look at what drives people to lose their moral compass in the pursuit of power. You will discover how the political spirit is the mastermind that forges alliances with the religious and Jezebel spirits to forward its own hidden agenda. This book will uncover political propaganda masquerading as a quest for the greater good.

The political spirit has been specifically assigned to block the establishment of the government of the Kingdom of God on the earth by instituting false government and corrupt political practices. It's the spirit behind the positioning and strife we see in earthly governments and behind divisions in the Church; it's the hidden mastermind using the spirit of Islam to spread terrorism and anarchy across the globe today. Because of its cunning ways, we will soon see a new, more insidious, and subtle form of terrorism blindside the world. If the Church doesn't stand up to act now, many will needlessly be lost.

The political spirit has been specifically assigned to block the establishment of the government of the Kingdom of God on the earth by instituting false government and corrupt political practices.

The purpose of this book is to equip you with supernatural perception in order to recognize, confront, and defeat this secret intelligence—whether in your personal life, family, workplace, church, city, or nation. Furthermore, you will learn the difference between false governing systems and the true government of God so that you will be able to walk out your Kingdom assignment to completion. We are moving into the age of divine government, and at this final frontier, the greatest enemy of our times is about to be exposed and dismantled. God wants to expose the origin, intent, expressions, and methods of this entity and to equip you with the wisdom to overcome it. When that takes place, the government of God will bring a greater expression of His Kingdom on earth. That means you will have the ability to release the Kingdom within you into your sphere of influence, into the very culture of our day. Muslims really seem to grasp this concept to a certain extent. They don't just want you to believe in Allah and Mohammad, but they want to occupy every platform of influence in government, education, banking, media, and technology (just to name a few) around the world. They want to change the very culture you live in and change the laws that govern it. We will discuss this in more detail later in the book.

Up until now, in this season of preparation, God has been protecting His people by an invisible ceiling. He desires to align His Body so that His Church can be prepared to defeat this hidden mastermind. The season for this ceiling to be removed is now. Once we understand how to deal with the political spirit operating in our midst, God can unleash His glory and infuse the light of His Kingdom into the darkest corners of the world. It is time for true government to be released once more; it is time for the government of God to be established—the place where God's will and tender mercies can once more flow without interference from the enemy.

It is time for true government to be released once more, it is time for the government of God to be established—the place where God's will and tender mercies can once more flow without interference from the enemy.

This is the heart of God concerning you: *"The Lord is not slack concerning His promise, as some count slackness, but is longsuffering toward us, not willing that any should perish"* (2 Pet. 3:9). Because He does not want you to be overcome by the world, He takes the time necessary to prepare you so that you will be in position to obtain His promise and fully partake of His glory. I know that many of you have been wounded and scarred by the work of the political spirit, but God wants you to know that it is time for you to be rejuvenated and healed; it is time for you to receive a new arsenal of weapons for fighting this destroyer. God is not through with you yet, and your mission has not been rescinded.

I believe we live in a time when God is calling each of us to move up beyond the invisible ceiling into a greater position of influence. (Get my book *Positioned to Bless: Secrets to Fulfilling your Divine Assignment*). It is the season for making strides in how we think and what we yield to. We need to understand God's ways so that we can get in step with His will as we enter the earth's last lap. In Psalm 25:4, David cried out to the Lord, *"Show me your ways...."* This should be our cry as well. Once you know the ways of God, you can begin to truly cooperate with Him. This is the season to come up higher; God will always call you up higher when He wants to speak something deeper to you.

I believe Hebrews 5:12-14 is speaking to the Church today:

For though by this time you ought to be teachers, you need someone to teach you again the first principles of the oracles of God; and you have come to need milk and not solid food. For everyone who partakes only of milk is unskilled in the word of righteousness, for he is a babe. But solid food belongs to those who are of full age....

We have become unskilled in the word of righteousness. In the time of battle, we are not postured and prepared as God's people to be able to deal with the opposition—we are not able to wield *"the sword of the Spirit, which is the word of God"* (Eph. 6:17). When you are able to rightly divide the word of truth (see 2 Tim. 2:15), God begins to open your eyes and show you His ways. God has divine strategies that He wants to reveal to enable you to defeat the enemy in this final hour.

My desire for you is that you would know the ways of God, not merely the acts of God. If you are only familiar with the acts of God, you will follow after acts—you will go wherever acts of God are happening. But if you know the ways of God, you are an act poised to happen.

We must understand the tides of our times and specifically the nature of the spiritual warfare taking place around us through the influence and deception of the political spirit. We must ensure that we are in step with the Holy Spirit and that no other spirit of this world—specifically the political spirit—corrupts our course or causes us to step falsely. Before we go any further about the political spirit and how to overcome it, I must first lay some significant foundations, recap the recent season we have been in, and help you to understand the strong man principle. Once we do that, then you will be ready to embark on a journey that will change your world forever. May God speak to you mightily through the message in this book. May it help equip you with the supernatural perception and divine strategies you need to defeat this enemy. He has great things in store for you in the days to come; may you meet each of them in the fullness of His grace.

Chapter 1

THE WAYS
OF GOD

*They sent their disciples to Him along with the
Herodians. "Teacher," they said, "we know You
are a man of integrity and that You teach the
way of God in accordance with the truth. You
aren't swayed by men, because You pay no
attention to who they are"* (Matthew 22:16 NIV).

It is tough to pick up a paper today and not read about some
new conflict somewhere in the world. Though the Cold War is
nearly two decades over, it didn't take long for other diametrically-
opposed worldviews to come head-to-head. Eons-old belief systems and governing structures that have coexisted for millennia
are now clashing on a global scale. West and East, Christianity
and Islam, democracy and terrorist totalitarianism stand poised to
define the sides of the next world war. However, disputes over
territory are no longer just geographical—nor are they simply

over political philosophies or religious practices. We are entering an age where the spiritual nature of our rivalries is more apparent than ever. As the Bible says,

> *We do not wrestle against flesh and blood, but against principalities, against powers, against the rulers of the darkness of this age, against spiritual hosts of wickedness in the heavenly places* (Ephesians 6:12).

What we are seeing today is certainly of biblical proportion, and only those who understand the true nature of today's turmoil will be equipped to successfully deal with it.

> **Only those who understand the true nature of today's turmoil will be equipped to successfully deal with it.**

These are critical times. These are defining times. The world's systems are in upheaval. But it is during such times of upheaval that we are given extraordinary opportunities to take new frontiers for our King. We are living in a period in history when a portal will be opened between time and eternity. God is about to sovereignly intervene in world affairs to forever change the destiny of all the peoples of the earth. It is a *kairos* time—a season appointed by God as a crossroad in the human story—and we need to be ready to take our part in it.

The modern Church is experiencing a major shift that will be felt in every arena and ripple to every corner of the globe. We are entering an era of seeing the Kingdom of God manifested; it is an entirely new season requiring a new level of discernment and alignment with the instructions of God. God wants His Church to walk in the power of His presence in order to release His Kingdom and its ways in the corporate and individual lives of believers and all those they touch in every level of society. He has dropped a plumb line into the midst of the Church and is calling His people to a higher standard so that they can walk in greater power and authority. It is a time of choosing to whom you belong and who you will follow—of making adjustments and crossing through that portal between time and eternity that separates God's Kingdom in Heaven from those of the earth. It is time to take hold of God's will with both hands and to bring it into our world for our times. More than any other period of history since Jesus walked the earth, the Kingdom of God is close at hand.

> **It is a time of choosing to whom you belong and who you will follow—of making adjustments and crossing through that portal between time and eternity that separates God's Kingdom in Heaven from those of the earth.**

Lining Up With the Will of God

Several years ago, the word of the Lord came to the Church calling for alignment. God began to speak to His people saying, "I want you to come into alignment with My Word, with My truth, and with My purposes. Align your vision. Align your hearts. Align your marriages. Align your finances. Align your character." It was an initial season of preparation for the coming age of divine government.

Then God began to drop His plumb line into the midst of His people—the standard to which He expected His children to align their lives. This plumb line was a greater presence of Jesus Himself. Today God is still aligning His Body to the perfect, heavenly plumb line of Jesus Christ. He is saying, "There is a plumb line, and I'm asking people to align what they have built with it—to align how they live, think, talk, and behave. I'm looking for alignment according to a standard that is *My* plumb line, one dropped down from Heaven and not created by human beings." You don't mess with God's plumb line. It's His divine order. People will not make a successful transition into the new era of God's government if they are not in alignment with God's plumb line.

Because of our lack of alignment, a divine ceiling has been hovering over the Church. Have you felt this ceiling in your life? Every time you try to push up higher, you feel like you hit your head against something impenetrable. You might have thought it was the devil hindering you, but it wasn't. It was God keeping you from getting into things that you were not yet ready for. There will need to be some pruning in your life—and in the Body of Christ in general—before this ceiling can be breached. And then the fruit can come—fruit like the Body of Christ has never seen before.

God is the master gardener and builder. He is building His living temple, fitly joined together. It is His workmanship—His great masterpiece. But He must also do things properly and in order. Before He can release us to the next level, we must be in alignment with His standards and will. If He allows us to break through this ceiling prematurely, we would be overcome because we are not yet ready to operate in the power required to succeed at that level. We must accomplish the work of this season before we can handle the challenges of the next.

God is aligning His people because He loves us, not because He desires to condemn us. Some think God has given up on them, but that is not true. God is bringing alignment because He has a corporate assignment for us—the very thing we feel destined in our hearts to accomplish. Some are ready now, but we must move forward together. Until God feels His Church is ready as a whole, we must be patient and continue preparing.

More Than Overcomers

God has shown me that, in previous seasons, because He taught His people to take new territory by battling the enemy, many have become stuck in the mindset of having to wrestle with the enemy at every turn. We have forgotten how powerful our God truly is. There are battles that He has already won on our behalf. We need only have Jesus speak the word as He did for the centurion. Yes, we had to learn about walking in the faith and authority that the apostles did in the book of Acts. Yet at the same time, God is still sovereign, and there are things He is doing that are beyond our faith and authority—there are things we simply need to fall in line with. To do this, we must clearly hear and obey the voice of His Spirit.

God has allowed us to relearn the elementary principles of faith because, for a time, the doctrine of God's sovereignty crippled the Church. There was an era during which God's sovereignty was preached as so absolute that you could hardly breathe without God's permission. If you died, it was His will; if you had a car accident, it was His will; if you developed cancer, it was His will. People believed that everything that happened was His will to the point that it seemed there was no reason to pray or even study the Bible. God was the cause of everything—your job was to accept every circumstance and try to understand what He was teaching you through each one. Experiencing suffering suddenly carried more weight than Scripture itself.

But this is not the true will of God—God wants covenant partners, not pawns. This is why God has been training His people in the word of righteousness and teaching them how to operate in His gifts. He has been revealing the degree of the spiritual authority that He has established within every believer and the unique callings that He has given every member of His Body. Now He is preparing us for even more. He is aligning His people to the plumb line of Heaven so that He can open its gates and let it flood the world. He is going to remove the ceiling and take His Church into a place where His glory can dwell in our midst.

God is aligning His people to the plumb line of Heaven so that He can open its gates and let it flood the world.

To be victorious in these last days, the Body of Christ will need to be carriers of the glory of God. This is no joke or boast. It is nothing to take lightly. We may sing about His glory, or casually talk about it, but carrying God's glory, or being present when the glory of God manifests, is a weighty thing. The glory of His presence is sweet and nice to a certain degree. But when you go beyond a light visitation of God's presence and move into a deeper habitation, your life must be divinely aligned—it must be plumb—or else that glory will lay you out cold, just as it did the priests inaugurating Solomon's temple in First Kings 8:11—*"The priests could not stand to minister because of the cloud, for the glory of the Lord filled the house of the Lord"* (ESV).

Despite God's patience, there will be some people who will not cross over into this new season of government—the season of God's glory being openly displayed in His Church. They will not be in a position to run, let alone stand, when God's presence is manifested. But there will be many who will be prepared and will run with endurance and carry God's presence into the darkest recesses of the earth.

These are the very things that you and I have been longing for. We've been praying and seeking His face for them. We've secretly desired in our hearts to see and know His presence openly—to meet Him face-to-face. This is why God has sent prophets to begin to bring understanding of the times. Second Chronicles 20:20 tells us, *"Believe in the Lord your God, and you will be established; believe His prophets, and you will succeed"* (ESV). Prophets around the world have been bringing these keys and insights to us over the last several years, preparing us for something that we are entering into right now—a whole new age—a whole new territory that we are going to be able to inhabit. In order to be part of it, we must understand and be willing to align our lives in accordance with God's divine government.

Past Failures

Of course, as you are reading this, you may be thinking that this is too "pie in the sky." It has been tried before. Great moves of God have swept the earth, and it all ended within just a few decades. David and Solomon established a holy nation unto God, but after their deaths, it was split in two. Jesus came and the apostles went out, and a hundred years later, the miracles were gone. John and Charles Wesley and George Whitefield started the Great Awakening and the Methodist church, but that movement is powerless today. William and Catherine Booth started the Salvation Army and swept the Gospel around the world, but now the Army is merely is a charitable organization that no longer holds the salvation of souls as its primary aim.

I know what you mean. As I was learning all of this, I asked the same questions while also doing all that I could to stay in step with what Jesus was calling His Church to become. And in the process, God began to give me a key that those past movements overlooked. It is the subject of this book.

The political spirit infiltrated and derailed each of those movements as their founders died and handed the reins on to the next generation. If we are to succeed where these others have failed, we must know how to deal with this spirit and defeat it in a way completely different from any spiritual warfare of the past. We must understand it in relation to our callings, take our positions of authority, and embrace God's divine mandates for our lives individually and for our communities. It is not a matter of resisting the devil as much as learning to submit to God in a new and more complete way. However, there are things you need to understand before we can start discussing this. You must first understand what God is doing in this next phase of His divine plan and learn to get in step with His ways.

God's government will be established as we align our lives to His divine order, first in our individual lives and then corporately.

Divine Mandates

God's government will be established as we align our lives to His divine order, first in our individual lives and then corporately. As we do that, we will position ourselves to be used of God to see a whole new level of dominion released. This is the era for end-time assignments to be unlocked. We are moving into a season of divine mandates and heavenly directives. This goes beyond operating in our areas of gifting or ministerial calling—this is on the level of strategically accomplishing tactical missions within the end-time battle plan of God. God is appointing His officers and commissioning His troops. You are moving into an era of deployment—a season of fulfillment—of actually accomplishing the eternal purpose that God has ordained for your life.

You are moving into an era of deployment—a season of fulfillment—of actually accomplishing the eternal purpose that God has ordained for your life.

Your personal fitness and preparation are vital to the success of the Body of Christ at work in the earth. When recruits join up, they first go to boot camp, where they are equipped and trained for battle. They are physically driven toward fitness, they are mentally challenged and prepared to make the right decisions under fire, and they are spiritually enabled to go toe to-toe with death and walk away unscathed. In the same way, everything in your life has been preparation and training for you to help you fulfill your God-given assignment. This developmental progression is what I have come to understand, from the study of Scripture and from experience, as a truly holy and divine process. It is the refining required to convert the lumpy clay (what you gave to Christ) into a vessel fit for honor and able to hold His life. It is a process that purifies your heart and exposes and refines out the impurities of your mind.

Like Moses, Joseph, David, and the other patriarchs, you will go through a refining process. They each had a sense of their calling, but it was distorted by their self-will. Only after long seasons in the wilderness were they able to acknowledge that God alone sustained their lives. They had to let go of self-rule and embrace God's rule—they had to be able to say as Paul did, *"...It is no longer I who live, but Christ who lives in me..."* (Gal. 2:20 ESV).

You may have lost sight of a vision or desire you once had. Perhaps you have lost heart because of the preparation and training that you have been through. But the Holy Spirit wants to remind you that God hasn't forgotten what He put in your heart. Instead, He has been refining the treasure that He has placed within you for your appointed season of destiny—*"...He who began a good work in you will carry it on to completion..."* (Phil. 1:6 NIV). Part of the preparation process is learning to let go and to rely on the hand of God to begin *and* finish the work that He has created in and for you—at all times *"looking unto Jesus, the author and finisher of our faith..."* (Heb. 12:2).

The Hand of God

You do not want to overlook "the hand of the Lord" that comes upon you for the purpose of fulfilling your God-given assignment. Whenever we deal with divine purposes and the uniqueness of God's call on people's lives, God's hand comes into operation. There will be a greater measure of God's presence and power as He establishes His will in the individual and corporate lives of His people. When I say corporate, I mean, the entire Body of Christ together—because divine purposes are bigger than any one person.

Your genuine call is not actually about you as much as it is about advancing a corporate purpose within God's Kingdom. God is doing something on a communal scale that you must get into alignment with. You will find that, just before you step into what God has called and destined you for, there will be a distinct moment in time when you will recognize that something in your life must change—a specific moment when a choice is presented and you have to make a decision. You will know that you have to make a change in your life in order to move on with God.

These are the adjustments you make as you align your life with God's plumb line—just as a chiropractor makes seemingly insignificant adjustments that bring correction and alignment to your spine. Perfect alignment is achieved one tiny modification at a time. The more aligned you become with God's Word, the more attuned you will become to the leading of His Spirit and the more clarity you will have about how to accomplish His will concerning your life.

Perfect alignment is achieved one tiny modification at a time.

The more aligned you become with God's Word, the more attuned you will become to the leading of His Spirit and the more clarity you will have about how to accomplish His will concerning your life.

Remember, revelation is progressive. The closer you get to your season, the more insight and understanding you will have. Revelation intensifies as you approach the time when God's purpose inside of you is about to come forth. You will have a lot of unanswered questions until you actually start doing the thing God has called you to accomplish. God has ordained it that way so that He can lead you in faith and show you how to trust Him. However, as you approach the season of your assignment, revelation will begin to unfold more rapidly.

We need to understand some important truths as we enter this new season. We can learn what pitfalls to avoid and how to flow with the Holy Spirit by looking at the experiences of the early Church. In Acts, we see early believers enter a new season of divine assignments and authority. In Acts 13:2, the Holy Spirit says, *"Now separate to Me Barnabas and Saul for the work to which I have called them."* Paul and Barnabas were both apostles by gifting and by calling before the foundation of the world. They were recognized and commissioned at an appointed time while they were yet prophets and teachers, but the gifting of an apostle had always been operating within them. Though Paul knew of his calling, he now has an apostolic assignment entrusted to him. God was calling him up to a new level, just as He is calling us today.

This is what is happening throughout the Body of Christ. We are moving into a season of commissioning and bestowing. God will commission you into your assignment, whether it is in business, government, education, ministry, or another arena that God has positioned you for. When you are commissioned, God's government and God's hand will back you. You'll start to see God's support in a measure that you haven't sensed it before. But don't fall into pride over it—it doesn't have as much to do with you as with your divine mandate.

Passing the Tests

By now you've probably already been through many tests and trials. You've been to the wilderness and been tested as Jesus was (see Luke 4:1). You will have demonstrated that you will not live by bread alone, but by every word that proceeds out of the mouth of God. You will have come to the place where, no matter what happens, you will trust in the Word of God and not in the world's resources. You will have passed what I call the "mammon test," proving that God—not money or worldly wealth—is your source.

You will have also passed the identity test. You will have had the opportunity to firmly establish who you are in Christ. Perhaps you cried out to God for revelation about His plan and intent for your life and heard Him say something like this: "My child, I love you with an everlasting love. I will never leave you nor forsake you. You are precious in my sight." Your response may have been, "Oh that's wonderful God! But what do You want me to do?" Then you heard God say, "I will always be by your side. Don't be afraid. Trust in Me, and I will set you on high." Again, you may have replied, "Thank you Lord, but what do you want me to do? What is my purpose?" And again you heard God say, "Remember my child, I am with you even unto the end. I love you with an everlasting love. I love you as much as I love Jesus." You entreated, "But Lord, isn't there anything I'm called to do?"

Now, why does God do this? It is because He doesn't want your identity to be replaced by your purpose. He knows how big your purpose is—whatever your purpose is, it is bigger than you think. God needs you to be affirmed and established in your identity so that you are one hundred percent assured of who you are in Him. You are defined by who He has made you to be in Christ; you find your identity because you are His child, not because of any special anointing or calling.

God doesn't want your identity to be replaced by your purpose.

When you get that settled, then He will begin to reveal purpose. And right before your purpose is revealed, your gifts will be awakened. You may notice that you are a gifted teacher or worship leader or youth worker. You may notice that you are gifted in business, finance, or leadership and think, "I'm going to build on this gift to bring glory to God." You begin to step out and doors will shut in your face. You ask, "Lord, what does this mean?" You will hear God say, "My child, don't build your life upon the gift because the gift will become an idol that keeps you from me." If you are like me, you will ask, "But Lord, how can I make this work? How can I make sense of what I am supposed to do?" That is when God will say, "Son, you need to know My ways. If you know My ways, you will not harden your heart."

The Bible tells us that the children of Israel hardened their hearts in this way: *"...It is a people who go astray in their hearts, and they do not know My ways"* (Ps. 95:10). The writer of Hebrews reminds us that *"they always go astray in their heart, and they have not known My ways"* (Heb. 3:10). Why were their hearts hardened? Self-deception hardened their hearts. Pride blinded them. They were deceived by their desires because they were ignorant of the ways of God.

You must know the ways of God if you are not going to be deceived as the children of Israel were. If you don't know the ways of God, you will not know why you are in the wilderness, or worse, that you are even in the wilderness! Your life will not make sense, and you will be tempted to become bitter. You won't understand how God can promise you something and then take you in a completely opposite direction. In addition, you will be dealing with the enemy at the same time that you are feeling powerless, vulnerable, and abandoned. To keep from letting your heart grow hardened, you need to understand what God is doing. You need to understand the way He trains you and prepares you for fruitfulness. You need to understand how He governs and how He speaks to you. Understanding His ways is the next key to standing your ground when the day of evil comes.

Knowing the Ways of God

God led the children of Israel into the wilderness to prove their hearts and to humble them. He did it as a reminder to the generations about His ways of developing people toward their potential: *"Remember how the Lord your God led you all the way in the desert these forty years, to humble you and to test you in order to know what was in your heart..."* (Deut. 8:2 NIV). In the New Testament, it was the Holy Spirit who led Jesus into the wilderness to be tempted by the devil. In Luke 4:1 we read, *"Then Jesus, being filled with the Holy Spirit, returned from the Jordan and was led by the Spirit into the wilderness."*

If you don't understand that testing and refining are part of the ways of God, you will think it was the devil that led you into the wilderness and isolated you. You will be cursing the devil when you should be checking your heart. The children of Israel weren't led into the desert either by the devil or to fight the devil, they were being tested on whether or not they would continue to trust God. Would they trust and obey God, or would they fall back on their own wisdom? They failed the test, but you don't have to if you look to Jesus and follow His example.

When you end up in the wilderness, you might be tempted to operate under a revelation that you received in a previous season. You might find yourself trying to use your authority to overpower the devil as you did in the past, when instead you should be submitting to God's authority and seeking out what He is trying to teach you in the wilderness. As the Bible says, *"Therefore submit to God. Resist the devil and he will flee from you"* (James 4:7). Don't miss the fact that God is after a heart submitted to Him and fail to see that it was the Holy Ghost that led you to this place for your edification and growth.

If you don't know the ways of God, you will most likely fall prey to a victim mentality, as did the children of Israel. You will feel that God has abandoned you or that He is punishing you or that you are destined to live out the rest of your days in the desert. You will say to yourself, "God isn't delivering me from the enemy here. He has forgotten about me. God called me to great-ness and gifted me and then left me in the wilderness at the mercy of the devil." Yet God is standing there, right next to you, telling you how much He loves you and how He will never leave you! He is telling you how precious you are to Him and that He loves you just as He does Jesus—yet you hear none of it because you are focusing on fighting the devil to overcome your circum-stances rather than getting quiet before God to hear what He is speaking to you. He sent you into the wilderness, just as He did Jesus, so that He could prepare you for the next phase of your mission.

When you understand God's ways, you will trust Him enough to believe what He has spoken to you. Understanding will give you the courage to live by every word that proceeds out of the mouth of God (see Matt. 4:4). This knowledge will give you the strength to stand in the day of temptation and to not compromise.

The Holy Spirit may lead you into the wilderness, but only you can keep yourself there.

The Holy Spirit may lead you into the wilderness, but only you can keep yourself there. You may build a house and set up a business in the wilderness. You may have witty inventions and ideas and use your gift in the wilderness to impress others who, like you, have chosen to reside there. You may even start a min-istry in the wilderness. You might begin to think that you are actually called of God to make your permanent home in the wilderness—that your purpose is to help other people make a better life in the wilderness. But in doing any of these things, you are missing God's best for your life and making what God meant as a passing phase of your development into a lifelong trial.

But God still won't give up on you. If you fail to pass the test the first time, then He will give you a retake. The Holy Spirit will begin to prompt you the next time the same test comes around again. I've been around that mountain more than once myself. I've seen some familiar landmarks that were there the time before. Whenever you see a pattern repeated in your life, pay attention. Often the pattern is in your blind spot, and you are about to face some tests that you failed before. In His love, God will try to get you to see that the test is coming again, and He will even use other people to help you see the pattern. This has happened to me more than once.

Several years ago, I was in business and partnered with various others as opportunities arose. That is a wonderful thing if you are called to do it. But God didn't call me to do that. I finally heard God saying, "Just like Abraham made a covenant with Me and did not make a covenant with the King of Sodom, so likewise I have called you not to make that kind of covenant. I have given you the seat of authority in the areas that I have called you to, and no man is to share the seat that I have given you." So I learned in my life to not make unnecessary covenants with other people.

Now this will not be the same for everyone. This is the instruction I received concerning the mandate and the call I have. I failed to heed this instruction twice before I learned this lesson though. Not recognizing the pattern cost me miserably. I had a lack of understanding of the way of God for my life. I had to face the same choice over and over until I passed the spiritual test behind it.

After those two failed tests, a man called me to say he loved my message about Ishmael. He said he wanted to give me $5 million plus royalties from the sale of my book—but in return, he would be allowed to put his company's name on everything to do with the message. He was a media mogul and wanted to produce a documentary on television. All I would have to do is allow him to attach his name to the message.

To complicate matters more, I had been praying and trusting God for millions of dollars to fulfill my assignment. People had prophesied that great doors of opportunity would open. However, I began to realize that I had been around this bend before. I knew in my spirit that I had failed this same test in the past by forming partnerships. I had failed a $30,000 test resulting from a partnership, and now this was a $5 million test. Somehow I knew this was not the will of God for me. I sensed in my spirit that this was an opportunity to pass that particular test once and for all, so I told the man "no." It felt odd because there was nothing wrong with the man or the arrangement. He was a good man—he was actually a Christian, so I wouldn't have been unevenly yoked. The business model made sense; it was fair and seemingly a win-win for all parties, but it just wasn't the will of God for my life. So I obeyed God and said, "no."

Now God didn't give me a detailed explanation of why I needed to turn this offer down; He just gave me a witness in my spirit. At the moment of decision, the Holy Spirit awakened in me and said, "Hey son, do you want to pass this one?" So I told the man, "Sir, I'm sorry. I cannot do that. I have to steward, like a Fed Ex deliverer, the message I have directly to the people it belongs to. No other name can be attached to this message except the name of Jesus Christ."

The man had also promised us some other exciting things that he would have been able to do. But as it turns out, we didn't need him to do any of it because God did it all better than this man ever could have done it. Should we be surprised?

When you pass these types of tests, you gain more authority. You begin to operate in a supernatural realm of authority in your life because you grow beyond worldly wisdom and the reach of the enemy's tactics to tempt and distract you. What I am sharing with you will save years of your life.

> **When you pass these types of tests, you gain more authority. You begin to operate in a supernatural realm of authority in your life because you grow beyond worldly wisdom and the reach of the enemy's tactics to tempt and distract you.**

If you know the ways of God, you will have discernment when it comes to the seasons of your life. Do you want to change your season? Then understand how the Holy Spirit is working with you and the lessons that God is trying to teach you. Recognize the tests in the season you are in. When you are able to identify them, you will be able to pass them. Don't compromise. Get lined up with God, and God will move you up the line.

> **Don't compromise. Get lined up with God, and God will move you up the line.**

The Nature of Spiritual Warfare

It is impossible to understand the Kingdom and government of God without having an understanding of God's ways. To understand and work within God's government, you have to attune your spiritual senses to His divine order. You have to develop acuity to God's sovereign rule.

Many times the enemy will try to use temptation to cause you to give into the lusts of your own flesh and create an unhealthy cycle to trip you up—he does this to non-Christians and Christians alike. The intent is for this cycle to create an open door for an evil spirit to attach itself to your life and keep you trapped through a mindset or destructive behavior pattern. At that point, you are not just dealing with an attitude or feeling but with a spirit that is operating in your life to try to destroy you and what God has called you to accomplish.

A religious spirit, for example, will make a person grow overly pious and legalistic, and in a gradual, step-by-step process, the person will go from being a true believer to a tool in the hand of the devil, distorting the truth to the point of destroying lives. It is what happens with cults such as the one led by Jim Jones, where hundreds drank poison thinking it was the will of God.

As the Bible says, there is nothing new under the sun (see Eccles. 1:9). This is why it is important to recognize and discern deceitful strategies and to overcome them. Without this skill and knowledge, good men and women are fooled everyday, thinking they are obeying God as they are being subtly manipulated and slowly taken off course by the slightest degree. At first no one notices, but then one day the good they were doing looks nothing like good at all. They have been deceived and blinded to the truth, and it will take a major work of God's grace to bring them back to the truth.

> **Without this skill and knowledge, good men and women are fooled everyday, thinking they are obeying God as they are being subtly manipulated and slowly taken off course by the slightest degree.**

Satan has demons that specialize in these tactics and thus become literally "spirits of" whatever that strategy is. This is what the Bible means when it talks about seducing spirits and doctrines of demons. It is important that you understand the difference between a personal enemy opposing you as an individual versus the deceitful strategies of satan opposing your assignment and the eternal purposes of God.

Most of the time, we deal with these strategies and attitudes on a more elementary level in our personal lives. If we can learn to recognize them when temptations are small, then we can render them powerless and move on in the purpose God has for us with power and divine authority.

This might seem obvious to some, but I have heard people give opinions about "God's will" without having any real biblical understanding of it. They are spouting age-old lies as if they were words from the Lord because they have fallen prey to subtle attitudes of pride, envy, or jealousy. As Paul wrote, these are the works of the flesh because they are things in our fallen nature that satan can use to trip us up (see Gal. 5:19). They are emotional buttons that he can push to get us to do what he wants. Even without the help of the enemy, our natural reasoning is most always self-justifying, or worse, self-promoting, and it leads to false governing systems—systems that are ultimately man-made and block the operation of the Kingdom and government of God in that sphere. This is what the political spirit uses to corrupt divine order. It creates false government that is contrary to God's sovereign rule, and it is not only deceptive, but also destructive.

We must be able to identify the work of the political spirit so that we can know how to address it. Before we go any further about the political spirit, it is important for you to understand the strongman principle and to know how to bind the "strong man."

Meditation Points

- In the Lord's prayer, we pray *"Your kingdom come. Your will be done on earth as it is in heaven"* (Matt. 6:10). When you pray that, what do you think of? How do you envision God's

Kingdom—a place where God's will is done on earth as easily as it is in Heaven—being spread around you?

- God wants covenant partners, not pawns. As God unleashes the next *kairos* for the earth—a time when His glory will return to His Bride—what will your part be? What is the mission that you feel God has placed in your heart for such a time as this?

- What obstacles have kept you from fulfilling what you sense God has called you to do? Are there alignment issues that you need to pray through and make right so that God's next phase of your mission can be revealed and released?

- How have you passed the wilderness test? The mammon test? The identity test?

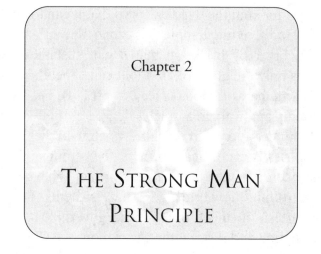

Chapter 2

THE STRONG MAN PRINCIPLE

But if I cast out demons by the Spirit of God, surely the kingdom of God has come upon you. [For] how can one enter a strong man's house and plunder his goods, unless he first binds the strong man... (Matthew 12:28-29).

The Kingdom of God has come upon us. We have been learning how to distinguish God's plumb line—and the vital importance of aligning our lives with the Word of truth. More than ever before, the Spirit is prompting us to make it a priority to seek God's Kingdom and His righteousness. There is an urgency to understanding and discerning the government of God and, by doing so, walking in a level of governmental authority not seen since the days of the apostles.

God has been preparing His Church—equipping and training His people—to be filled to overflowing with His honor and glory.

The filling is for you; the overflow is so that it can touch the lives of others. God's living temple has gone through the fires of refinement, brick by brick, so that it can sustain His glory—because it is only the glory of God that can expel the gross darkness at work in the world today (see Isa. 60:1-3). The Church will need to rise up and walk in a greater degree of righteousness—or divine alignment—to overcome the enemy of her future, the political spirit. The political spirit is the strong man working behind the scenes to gain power over spiritual and natural territories by controlling the world's governing systems. This spiritual enemy manifests in the form of false government, which has reaped deception and destruction throughout the Church and the world. It is the cunning spirit behind every corrupt governing system—and it can only be displaced by the true government of God.

Tragically, this spirit has operated within the Body of Christ as easily as it has anywhere else. Because of this, God is calling us to dismantle the influence of this spirit first within our own lives, then in our churches, and then in our nations. This must not only be displaced through divine strategies of faith, knowledge, and prayer, but it must also be replaced with the government of God's Kingdom. This strong man always raises its head as a government that ultimately is against God's blessings flowing to its people, even though it looks like it has the best interests of the people at heart. In order to make sure the false doesn't return, you must replace it with the true.

As God establishes true apostolic government, the political spirit that has taken hold in the Church will be exposed. When you deal with God's government, you deal with the hand of the Lord. When the hand of the Lord is in operation, the false things will be exposed and rendered powerless. Before we are able to identify and expose the political spirit, however, we must first understand the significance of a strong man.

What is a Strong Man?

A strong man, by definition, is a political leader, a military leader, or someone with jurisdictional power, control, or authority who is influenced by the political spirit. This person might not necessarily have legal or positional authority, but they have imposed their influence and control over a territory or region—they have established their authority, whether it is legitimate or not, over a specific area.

For example, Manuel Noriega, who was a general in Panama, was dubbed "The Strong Man of Panama." Even though he was not the president and did not have what we would consider the highest position in the nation, he actually dominated the region of Panama. He was the ruler, controller, power, and influence over that region and as a result went down in history as "Panama's Strong Man." He could not be displaced except through a stronger political force. So, in 1990, he was bound and brought to trial by the government of the United States for his human rights violations. In 1992, he was sentenced to 40 years in prison, where he remains today. Interestingly, even a higher authority convicted him when, in May of 1990, he gave his life to Jesus Christ.[2]

Let's look at a biblical illustration of a strong man. In Matthew 12, Jesus, the ultimate strong man, had just ousted a demon from a blind and mute man. The people in the area were amazed and began worshiping Jesus as the Son of David. The

Pharisees became jealous and accused Him of witchcraft saying, *"This fellow does not cast out demons except by Beelzebub, the ruler of the demons"* (Matt. 12:24). In other words, they questioned what authority had given him jurisdiction over the demon, presuming that it could have only been the ruler of demons. It is in the next few verses that we are introduced to the strong man principle. In Matthew 12:25-26, Jesus declares:

> *Every kingdom divided against itself is brought to desolation, and every city or house divided against itself will not stand. If Satan casts out Satan, he is divided against himself. How then will his kingdom stand?*

Notice that He uses the concept of a kingdom—in this case the kingdom of darkness—or it could be a city, a house, or a nation—to explain that any entity divided against itself it cannot endure. He goes on to clarify that if satan casts out satan, then his kingdom could not stand. It would self-destruct. Jesus is trying to make obvious the fact that He is binding the enemy by no power other than that of the Spirit of God.

He goes on to say:

> *And if I cast out demons by Beelzebub, by whom do your sons cast them out? Therefore they shall be your judges. But if I cast out demons by the Spirit of God [Luke 11:20 says "with the finger of God"] surely the kingdom of God has come upon you* (Matthew 12:27-28).

Jesus is making clear that He is casting out the devil by a higher governing authority—by the Kingdom of God that is above the kingdom of darkness. This is the evidence that the finger—or hand—of God is in operation.

The next statement Jesus makes succinctly states the strong man principle. In Matthew 12:29, Jesus asks, *"How can one enter a strong man's house and plunder his goods, unless he first binds the strong man?"* What he is saying is, unless you deal with the chief authority, the governing spirit, the one who has control or influence over a house, a city, a nation, or a region—until you bind or render that strong man harmless and void of power—you will be powerless before it. You can't go into a house or city or kingdom and take control of that territory until you first bind or defeat the strong man in charge there.

> **You can't go into a house or city or king-dom and take control of that territory until you first bind or defeat the strong man in charge there.**

Luke 11:21-22 interprets Jesus' explanation this way: *When a strong man, fully armed, guards his own palace, his goods are in peace. But when a stronger than he comes upon him and over-comes him, he takes from him all his armor in which he trusted, and divides his spoils.* We know that Jesus is stronger than all. He is the strong man of the universe. Now think about that in the context of this verse: *"...Christ in you, the hope of glory"* (Col. 1:27). The Jesus in you, the Christ in you, has called you to unique areas—whether it's a city, a house, or a region—areas where a strong man is usually, on some level, working against the plan of God.

For example, in your personal areas of influence, you have full jurisdiction to protect your family or your business interests from the schemes of the enemy. The enemy has no legal authority to interfere with what you are working on in your jurisdiction. But what if you go to Saudi Arabia and say, "You know, today I feel like taking out the strong man holding the Muslim world in bondage"? Does it work that way? No. First you must have that type of governmental authority granted to you by God, based on your call, which is a corporate assignment that will always be bigger than who you are or what you can do alone. This type of assignment is for taking new territory for God's Kingdom. There are governmental assignments that go way beyond the sphere of influence that most of us are used to, or able to understand, but we will see more of this type of pioneering authority being imparted in the lives of ordinary—soon to be extraordinary—Christians.

This is the *kairos* we are embarking on as the Body of Christ. We will begin to see the advancement of God's Kingdom like no one has yet seen on earth. This will happen to an increasingly greater degree as God's government is established, because as the government of the Kingdom of God comes upon us, we will be in a position to take greater authority over the enemy and take new territory. As the hand of God begins to move in the Church, the strong man will be exposed. It is that same governmental authority that will enable the Church to overtake and bind the strong man wherever he is revealed.

From a spiritual perspective, we see this in Ephesians 6:10-11: *"Finally, my brethren, be strong in the Lord and in the power of His might. Put on the whole armor of God, that you may be able to stand against the wiles of the devil."* A key to getting in position is putting on the armor of God. It is the process of alignment.

Stand therefore, having girded your waist with truth, having put on the breastplate of righteousness, and having shod your feet with the preparation of the gospel of peace; above all, taking the shield of faith with which you will be able to quench all the fiery darts of the wicked one. And take the helmet of salvation, and the sword of the Spirit, which is the word of God (Ephesians 6:14-17).

We are talking about spiritual alignment—*For we do not wrestle against flesh and blood, but against principalities, against powers, against the rulers of the darkness of this age, against spiritual hosts of wickedness in the heavenly places* (Eph. 6:12). In other words, we don't war against humans; we war against the spirits or demonic strategies corrupting them; we war against principalities, powers, rulers of darkness, and wickedness in high places. The forces at work against the Church—and every member of the Body of Christ—are in the spirit realm. Something is always vying for control behind what we can see in the natural realm. Many times we encounter situations that are not about people but are about the spirits that are influencing those people—they are using them like pawns in a chess game against you or against your assignment in life.

Let me give you an example of a strong man at work in a certain region against a local church and the people of God. There was a pastor who was the leader of one of the largest churches in Canada. This pastor had a national voice and great authority in the city and region where he ministered. He was highly anointed and called by God. Yet somehow he fell into sin, into a place of immorality, and eventually had to step down from his position as a leading minister in Toronto. Another pastor was sent to take his place and the people in the church thought the problem was solved. After all, the immoral person had been removed and replaced with a person of integrity and character.

To make a long story short, the new pastor fell into the sin of immorality as well, and so did the third pastor and the fourth. Every pastor after the original pastor fell into some sort of immorality that forced him to step down. This is an example of a strong man not being dealt with. A governing spirit behind that ministry had taken position and authority in that church and then preyed upon those pastors' weaknesses until each pastor ultimately fell.

Now you might be thinking those men were just weak, but that's not really the case. The Bible says that we are all fallible. The sin nature resides within the flesh of every person. Even though we have all been given victory over that sin nature in Christ Jesus, there is still an enemy seeking to destroy us. This is why we are told in First Peter 5:8, *"Be sober, be vigilant; because your adversary the devil walks about like a roaring lion, seeking whom he may devour."* The key is discerning where and how the adversary is working. There was a spirit behind the scenes that took advantage of each pastor's weakness and was, therefore, able to gain authority and control in that church. But the power or principality—the spiritual host of wickedness in high places—was never dealt with; the erring pastors were continually removed, but the strong man was untouched.

Unless the strong man is identified, it cannot be exposed, and unless it is exposed, it cannot be displaced.

Unless the strong man is identified, it cannot be exposed, and unless it is exposed, it cannot be displaced. True governmental authority must come forth throughout the Church to bind and replace the strong man at work against every kingdom assignment. Few who have given their lives for the Gospel's sake did so with the intention of falling into sin. They had to be directly challenged by a political spirit—a strong man—over the region and tempted to the point that they were overcome.

Binding the Strong Man

Positionally, we have been given every victory in Christ. But we are only able to walk in that victory to the extent of our revelation of the authority that we possess and abide in through Christ. The same authority that Jesus used when He walked the earth belongs to the Church today. Jesus bound the strong man, took authority over him, spoiled him openly, and rendered him useless, harmless, and ineffective through the cross. *"Having disarmed principalities and powers, He made a public spectacle of them, triumphing over them..."* (Col. 2:15). God then exalted Jesus to his right hand and caused us to be not only complete in Christ but also to be seated with Him in heavenly places far above principalities, powers, and rulers of darkness (see Eph. 1-2).

There is a difference between personal authority and corporate authority. Personal authority is about your personal life and the extent of your influence. Corporate authority has to do with the domain of your unique Kingdom assignment on behalf of the King and His domain. The government of the King is what protects you on a personal level and backs you in your Kingdom assignment on a corporate level. On a personal level, you have every right to take authority over the devil and over the kingdom of darkness in your family, in your home, on your property, or in your business—that is, if you are walking in obedience to God and submitted to His authority in all of those areas. However, you do not necessarily have corporate authority to bind a strong man that is greater than your house. You have been given dominion in Christ Jesus over whatever concerns your life but not over areas outside your personal sphere of influence, such as a city, a church, or a nation—unless you are specifically called out and anointed by God for that purpose.

Personally, I was born in the Islamic Republic of Pakistan. The strong man over that nation is the political spirit behind Islam. You can't go into Pakistan and command that strong man to leave the nation unless God has granted you specific authority over it. This type of authority would be on the scale of Moses usurping Pharaoh. Most people don't operate in that degree of governmental, corporate authority.

If God did send you to Pakistan, you would operate under an umbrella of divine personal protection while you were there. However, until He decided to give you authority to bind and isolate the strong man over the nation of Pakistan, you wouldn't be able to remove or overcome it to set all of the people under that spirit's domain free.

> **This pattern of defeat could be a strong man or governing authority working against you, either on a personal level, with respect to your goals, or on a corporate level, with respect to the assignment God has given you.**

Having said that, let's look at where you do have jurisdiction—over in the sphere of your own life. You have probably identified patterns that continually repeat themselves in your life. You wonder why you keep visiting the same situations over and over again. You feel you are just about to make it when you are defeated by the same obstacles or limitations. This pattern of defeat could be a strong man or governing authority working against you, either on a personal level, with respect to your goals, or on a corporate level, with respect to the assignment God has given you. You might have to confront and identify a strong man that God wants you to overcome and gain victory over it just so that other people in your situation can be brought to freedom in that area.

For example, let's say you're struggling with an addiction in your life. Your father struggled with addiction, your grandfather struggled with an addiction, and now you're struggling with addictions, and you find you cannot break them. This is where you need to come to Jesus, the strong man of the universe, and allow His power and authority to reign in that situation. Recognize the root—or spirit—behind a problem that may have been operating in your family for generations. Come to Jesus and proclaim His Word and tap into the God-given authority that you have to destroy the root of this spiritual force working to sabotage your success. Take authority so that you can get victory over the strong man in your personal life.

When we talk about a city, a nation, a region, or any corporate assignment that you might have in the public arena—whether it's in the marketplace, government, or ministry—anywhere you believe God has divinely placed you—and you feel there is something that is opposing your purpose there, it's important that you identify what it is and begin to get wisdom from God so that you can deal with it. My hope is that, as you read this book, not only will you become familiar with what a strong man is, but you will also understand how to gain total victory over it.

> **I believe God wants to raise you up as a stronger person in Christ—to strengthen you to rise above the strong man of darkness or evil that you are encountering in your life today.**

I believe God wants to raise you up as a stronger person in Christ—to strengthen you to rise above the strong man of darkness or evil that you are encountering in your life today. You *"have [already] defeated and overcome them [the agents of the antichrist], because He Who lives in you is greater (mightier) than he who is in the world"* (1 John 4:4 AMP). Remember, you do not wrestle against flesh and blood, but against principalities, powers, and rulers of darkness (see Eph. 6:12). Remember too that you are seated with Christ in heavenly places *"far above all principality and power and might and dominion..."* (Eph. 1:21), and that you have been entrusted with a heavenly assignment that needs to be realized on the earth.

You might be asking, "But why should I continually have to overcome the enemy when Jesus has done it once and for all?" Paul gives this encouragement in Romans 16:19-20: *"...I want you to be wise about good things and pure about sinful things. God, Who is our peace, will soon crush Satan under your feet..."* (NLV). Yes, Jesus already conquered the enemy, but as you take your place in Christ and obey the assignment upon your life, you will learn to walk in the authority that has been granted you. You are called to be stronger than the strong man that is opposing you in your life today.

> [This] *is the fellowship of the mystery, which from the beginning of the ages has been hidden in God...to the intent that now the manifold wisdom of God might be made known by the church to the principalities and powers in the heavenly places* (Ephesians 3:9-10).

Breaking Free From Bondage

Have you ever felt that you have greatness in your heart—so much potential—so many dreams and visions that God has placed in your spirit? Have you ever heard prophetic words concerning your life, written them down, and kept them folded in your Bible to read and reread every chance you get? Perhaps you have meditated in prayer and gotten a sense of what God has deposited in you, yet you continually feel like you're confined or constrained somehow—you have not yet been released to do what you have been called to do. Do you ever feel frustrated about not being able to fulfill the call that you sense God has placed on your life?

Confinement can present itself in many different ways. Maybe the constraint is financial—perhaps there is no visible provision for the vision that God has given you. Maybe you are feeling confined by the position you find yourself in—perhaps it is not where you sense God has called you to be. Maybe He has called you to go to a particular nation or city or region, giving you a heart for a certain group of people, yet you remain in a place where you cannot fulfill your destiny to minister among those people. There are so many things that can hold you back. You want to break free, but circumstances keep you from doing it day after day.

Let me give you an example of confinement from my own life. From the time I came to know the Lord, I felt a sense of destiny in my heart. I was carrying a burden for the nations in my spirit. It was the winter of 1994, and I was living in Brampton, Ontario in Canada. It was one of the coldest winters ever recorded in Canada. I had just recently come to Jesus as a former Muslim. This is the greatest sin that any Muslim can commit. Somehow my family found out that I was hanging around Christians, and they feared that this would compromise my Muslim heritage.

During this time, I was living in a rental home owned by my family. I was fixing up the house so that we could secure better tenants. One day, I pulled up in my 1987 Nissan Sentra and discovered that the locks had been changed. They didn't even know that I had come to know Jesus, but they had already given power of attorney to a friend to sell the house that I was living in. I was suddenly homeless and without a family to go to for help.

I had my car and my life in boxes in the backseat, so I would sleep sitting up at night. I would find a parking lot full of parked cars so that I could camouflage myself in the hopes that no one would notice me sleeping in my car. I turned the heat on in the car until it warmed up, and then I turned it off and slept until I woke up again. This is what I did night after night. I slept in short intervals, showered at the YMCA, and sometimes went into the bathroom at McDonald's to shave and compose myself. I was doing my best. That car was my home. Now I can jokingly say that my car was my motor home—it had a motor and it was my home.

It was the coldest winter in 20 years, yet I had such joy. God had given me a destiny. He had placed a vision in my heart. Yes, I was confined by circumstances, but the fact that I knew Jesus was of more worth than my circumstances or my environment. I had every Muslim, Hindu, Sikh, and atheist making fun of me. Some would say, "You know, you have compromised by turning your back on the God of Islam, and that's why God is judging you, and that's why you're living in a car." I remember saying to them, "I only know one thing; whether I live in a car or live in a mansion, Jesus is the Son of God." The fact that I could be in personal relationship with the Son of God, and through that relationship, *be* a son of the Father, brought about a rest and a joy that was—and is—inexplicable. I had the profound revelation that it was more valuable to know Him than anything else.

When you get to that place where God becomes your priority—when all else has been stripped away from you, yet you are able to find contentment in the knowledge of your Savior—then you will know the peace that transcends understanding. It's all about becoming what God has called you to be rather than doing the thing God has called you to do. Once you get that into your heart, your mindset will come into alignment with the nature of God's truth for your life. Who you are is more important than the position you are called to fill. Suddenly you will begin to get into a posture and a position in your life where nothing can hold you back. Yes, there will be times of discouragement and isolation, but never despair. This is how the call of God is forged.

When you get to that place where God becomes your priority—when all else has been stripped away from you, yet you are able to find contentment in the knowledge of your Savior—then you will know the peace that transcends understanding.

The Bible says in Genesis that Abraham was called alone (see Isa. 51:2). The Scripture further illustrates how Jacob was left alone on the backside of a mountain and wrestled with God (see Gen. 32:24). If you're called of God, then one day you will either be called alone or you will be left alone. There will be a season of isolation in your life where no one will be able to relate to you—no one will be able to understand where you are coming from—but that is the season where you will learn to depend wholly on the love of God. That is the season where you will come to grips with your identity—where you will change who you are to become who God has made you to be. That is the season when you will acknowledge that your past does not define you—your pain does not define you—only what Jesus did on the cross defines you. You are defined only by who you have become in Christ as you go from glory to glory.

Romans 8:37 (NIV) says, *"...We are more than conquerors through Him who loved us."* This is the place that you begin to conquer through love. I believe that, the more of His love that you know, the more you will conquer in your life. Grace will get you through the problem, and faith will give you the victory in an event, but it is love that will make you more than a conqueror. Love is your state of being. "More than a conqueror" reveals who you are—it's not just talking about a temporary victory over a single event, but it's the definition of who you are, regardless of your circumstances.

Paul states in Romans 8:18, *"For I consider that the sufferings of this present time are not worthy to be compared with the glory which shall be revealed in us."* I believe the Spirit of God wants to reveal the greatness that He has deposited in your heart. God wants you to be released from the place of your imprisonment so that you are able to break free from every limitation—and bind every strong man opposing God's call upon your life. He wants to move you into a situation where you can recognize that you are sitting in a position of function and authority to fulfill the assignment for which you have been placed on the earth.

Opposition is certain. Learn to recognize it and overcome it with the righteousness of God at work in you—for *"...those who receive abundance of grace and of the gift of righteousness will reign in life through the One, Jesus Christ"* (Rom. 5:17).

Meditation Points

- A strong man is a political leader, a military leader, or someone who has jurisdictional power, control, or authority and is influenced by the political spirit. Have you seen this spirit at work in your workplace, church, city, or nation? How did it operate? What false policies were set up that counteracted releasing God's Kingdom in that place?

- Are there patterns of defeat in your life that you need to overcome? Ask God to expose these patterns to you so that you can recognize them. Then pray for God's wisdom for how to get victory over these situations.

• Have you ever felt that you have greatness in your heart—so much potential—so many dreams and visions that God has placed in your spirit? Have you ever heard prophetic words concerning your life, written them down, and kept them folded in your Bible to read and reread every chance you get? Take a look at those now and ask God to show you how He plans to renew them.

Endnotes

1. *Biography: "Manuel Noriega: The Rise and Fall of Panama's Strong Man,"* A&E Home Video, April 25, 2006.

2. Noriega's profession of faith in Jesus Christ, in 1990, and his baptism, in 1992, are chronicled in "The Conversion of Manuel Noriega," *American Rehabilitation Ministries*, www.arm.org/noriega.htm (accessed 27 August 2008).

Chapter 3

THE LEAVEN
OF HEROD

*Jesus [repeatedly and expressly] charged
and admonished them, saying, Look out;
keep on your guard and beware of the leaven
of the Pharisees and the leaven of Herod
and the Herodians* (Mark 8:15 AMP).

Probably, in some seasons in your life, it has seemed like you have had some victory. You encountered some challenges, even some spiritual warfare, and recognized a particular spirit or strategy of the enemy working against you—you may have even felt that you were about to be derailed from your assignment— but then you got victory over it. And yet, not too much later, that same principality that you had previously overcome resurfaced somewhere else. Why didn't you get a genuine, sustainable victory over it? You got so close to breaking through to the next level, but suddenly you found yourself fighting the same battle again.

Some of you have seen this happen in an organization that you are a part of, in your business, or even in your own home. You may feel like a failure or a fool, but I'm telling you that this is something that no one is immune to. It is something that I have seen on a regular basis with people from various levels of faith in God. There is a reason you are not getting permanent victory, and it has to do with the strong man principle. It has to do with the political spirit, which is the core and very essence of this spiritual strategy. The political spirit *is* the strong man—and until you deal with the underlying political spirit, you will never get lasting victory. Why? Because one of the characteristics of the political spirit is that it never works alone and usually works in the background. This is why, when you get power over something, it is able to come back again—you have conquered the "front man" spirit, but the political spirit has effectively evaded you because you never recognized that it was the hidden mastermind behind it all.

Tag-Team Spirits

In Mark 8:15, Jesus makes this statement: *"Take heed, beware of the leaven of the Pharisees and the leaven of Herod."* This is a command from the Lord. It would do us well to understand exactly what Jesus means by the "leaven of the Pharisees and the leaven of Herod." Jesus identifies two types of leaven— one religious and the other political. Now a leavening agent is something used to lighten or puff up bread. The leaven reacts with the starch while heat and moisture trigger the production of a gas, which becomes trapped in bubbles. While baking, the gas expands and dissipates, leaving air pockets or holes in the dough, giving bread its sponge-like texture. In other words, it causes the dough to expand and the bread to be soft.

When Jesus talks about the leaven of the Pharisees, He is talking about the pharisaical spirit, or a religious spirit. This is the same spirit that blinds pious leaders to the heart of God through legalism. They get so caught up in the law and their interpretations of it that they no longer know God as a loving, merciful Father, but only as a righteous judge. What did Jesus mean by the leaven of Herod, however? The leaven of Herod refers to the political spirit—or strong man—that we have been talking about.

We don't hear much about the life and lineage of Herod, other than that he was king of Judea during the time of Christ. Most don't know that the Herodian Dynasty spanned five generations and lasted nearly 140 years. It was a dynasty that emerged as a result of a series of calculated political alliances beginning with Herod the Great's grandfather, Antipas, who was appointed governor of Edom by the Jewish ruler Alexander Jannaeus. Antipas' son, Antipater the Idumaean, was appointed procurator of Judea by Julius Caesar in 47 B.C. Antipater appointed his two sons, Phasael and Herod, to be governors of Jerusalem and Galilee respectively. And in 37 B.C., the Roman Senate elected Herod "king of the Jews" and made him sole ruler over all of Judea. As such, he became known as Herod the Great. When Herod the Great died, the kingdom was divided between his three sons, Herod Archelaus, Herod Philip, and Herod Antipas, who he made ruler of Galilee. His grandson, Herod Agrippa I, reunited the kingdom and his great grandson, Agrippa II, ruled until his death in A.D. 92, ending the Herodian dynasty.

Now, what is especially interesting about Herod is that he descended from Edom. His father, Antipater the Idumaean, was an Edomite. *Idumea* was the Roman word for Edom, the southern region of Judea, also identified as Mount Seir in the Bible. When you see prophecies about Mount Seir, you will know that they are in regard to this group of people emanating from the territory of Edom. This point of origin is significant because it tells us that Herod's ancestors were descendents of Esau. In Genesis 36:8-9, we read, *"Esau dwelt in Mount Seir. Esau is Edom...the father of the Edomites in Mount Seir."* Around 140-130 B.C., the nation of Israel overtook Edom and forced them to convert to Judaism. They told the Edomites—those who were born of Esau—to either become Jews or to leave. Many of them stayed and became Jews, but they were Jews by name only, not by heritage or religious conviction.

This was the cultural and political climate at the time of Herod. Political Jews—also considered Hellenistic Jews—with an Edomite heritage, aligned themselves with Herod and were commonly referred to as Herodians. The Herodians were an active political party who supported a theocracy; some of them even believed Herod to be the Messiah. They allied with the Pharisees in plotting against Jesus. In the Amplified Bible version of Mark 8:15, we read: *"Beware of the leaven of the Pharisees and the leaven of Herod and the Herodians."*

If we look closely at Herod, we can begin to see how the political spirit operates.

If we look closely at Herod, we can begin to see how the political spirit operates. Herod had a political agenda from the beginning. He undermined the authority of the priestly dynasty, known as the Hasmoneans, which had ruled in that region for generations. The Hasmoneans were a priestly family who led the Jews in conquering Edom in 140 B.C., forcing the Edomites to abide by Jewish law. Herod used his alliance with Rome to put down any Hasmonean uprising. In 40 B.C., when the Hasmonean, Antigonus, tried to take the throne with the help of the Parthians, Herod fled to Rome where he formed an alliance with Mark Antony. Mark Antony formally installed him as king of Judea. Herod returned with a Roman army and had Antigonus executed. He then attempted to legitimize his position by marrying Marianme I, a Hasmonean princess, after conveniently exiling his first wife and child. He didn't stop there. To secure his position once and for all, he conspired to have the last Hasmonean heir murdered. And just to be sure he was accepted by the religious priesthood, he married Marianme II, the daughter of Simon the High Priest, to gain favor with the Jews.

Herod was an expert at establishing control through political alliances. After acquiring the backing of Rome, Herod wanted favor with the priests and Pharisees because he wanted to leave his mark on the Jewish temple. Historically, we know that Herod was a developer of grand public works and magnificent buildings. He built the Herodium, a beautiful, prestigious building. He expanded the second temple, which Jesus prophesied would be destroyed, as it was, interestingly enough, in A.D. 70. The famous Wailing Wall that still stands in Jerusalem, along the western side of the courtyard, was part of Herod's expansion.

Herod knew that religious and Jewish law required that anything to do with the temple had to be done through the Levites and priests. As a result, according to the historian, Josephus,

Herod employed one thousand priests to work on his behalf in expanding the temple, which ultimately became known as "Herod's Temple."[1] Herod was able to use and prostitute the priests while giving the appearance of respectfully adhering to Jewish customs and Levitical laws yet acting for his own personal power and political ambition. The spirit behind this motive is what I call the *Herodian spirit*, which is simply a unique expression of the political spirit.

What the Herodian spirit does is to politically use religion to further its agenda. It is the same tactic used by the spirit behind Islam, and it is taking hold in the final frontier of the western Church. Herod had a history of making alliances with religious leaders in order to gain more power. He also used these alliances to protect himself. In Matthew chapter two, you can see how this operates:

> *Now after Jesus was born in Bethlehem of Judea in the days of Herod the king, behold, wise men from the East came to Jerusalem, saying, "Where is He who has been born King of the Jews? For we have seen His star in the East and have come to worship Him."*

> *When Herod the king heard this, he was troubled, and all Jerusalem with him. And when he had gathered all the chief priests and scribes of the people together, he inquired of them where the Christ was to be born.*

> *So they said to him, "In Bethlehem of Judea, for thus it is written by the prophet:*

> *'But you, Bethlehem, in the land of Judah, Are not the least among the rulers of Judah; For out of you shall come a Ruler Who will shepherd My people Israel.' "*

Then Herod, when he had secretly called the wise men, determined from them what time the star appeared. And he sent them to Bethlehem and said, "Go and search carefully for the young Child, and when you have found Him, bring back word to me, that I may come and worship Him also" (Matthew 2:1-8).

Herod is smart enough to know that these wise men are pure of heart. He believes the prophecy and becomes concerned that he could lose his throne to this child. So what does he do? He runs to the Pharisees, the Chief Priests, and the scribes and has a private meeting with them. He tells them that he believes the prophecy concerning the birth of a king and wants to know where he will be born. He wants to know everything about him. The religious leaders are flattered to help Herod learn more about the Messiah. They probably think the Kingdom of God is expanding—the Jewish tradition and the Law of Moses are moving forward. The King of Judea came to them wanting to know what the prophets were saying—the Great Herod has come inquiring about the Word of God!

So the religious leaders confide to Herod that the true King of the Jews will be born in Bethlehem. Herod says, "Isn't that wonderful!" and pats them on the back. Herod understands that it is the season for this king's coming, because of the prophecies he heard from the wise men, but doesn't say a word about what he knows to the Pharisees. Herod plays dumb when he goes to speak with them and asks them to tell him everything they know.

Have you ever experienced this in your own life? You share all of the revelation you have, and you think you are making a difference—but you end up sharing it with someone who has a hidden motive. Herod's hidden motive was to kill this king while he was still a baby. He received a prophetic word, believed it, and attempted to use it to accomplish his own goal. His hidden agenda—his primary motivation—was simply to protect his own interests by eliminating the opposition.

> **The political spirit always has a hidden agenda that you will not be able to discern with your natural senses.**

That is the first thing I want you to notice about a political—or Herodian—spirit. It always has a hidden agenda that you will not be able to discern with your natural senses. Whether this spirit is operating through an individual or an organization, it will always be more interested in your prophetic word than even you are. You will be impressed by how seriously such a person is taking your divine insight to heart. The Pharisees are deceived by what appears to be humility and invested concern when Herod comes to them asking, "Please share with me these divine truths and what the prophets are saying about this king of yours."

> **The political spirit always creates alliances.**

The second thing to notice is that Herod meets privately with the Pharisees and creates an alliance. The political spirit always creates alliances. Herod—or better said, the political spirit motivating him—creates an alliance with the Pharisees through the political spirit's alliance with the religious spirit. It's a political alliance with the religious leaders.

After fooling the religious leaders into supporting and informing him, Herod goes to the wise men and meets with them privately. He does not want the Pharisees to have the information that was supplied to him by the wise men who saw the star. And he does not want the wise men to know what the Pharisees taught him about the prophecies concerning this coming King. He separates them and has secret meetings with each. After all, knowledge is power, and Herod wants to keep all of the power in his court. If he had only been interested in finding out about this new king so that he could properly honor Him, he would have called a joint meeting and openly asked what anyone knew about this prophetic event. But since that is not the case, the only way he can keep control of both groups is to keep them from communicating with one another.

Herod also has enough sense to realize that the wise men are of pure heart—unlike the Pharisees. So he plays innocent with them. He tells them, "Go and find out where this king is. You have the king's blessing backing you. I will even finance your trip if you return to tell me where he is so that I, too, can worship him." So with the purest of hearts, they head off carrying treasure: frankincense, myrrh, and gold to bestow upon the newborn king when they find Him.

And he sent them to Bethlehem and said, "Go and search carefully for the young child and when you have found him, bring back word to me, that I may come and worship him also." When they heard the king, they departed; and behold, the star which they had seen in the East went before them, till it came and stood over where the young child was. When they saw the star, they rejoiced with exceedingly great joy. And when they had come into the house, they saw the young child with Mary his mother, and fell down and worshiped him. And when they had opened their treasures, they presented gifts to him: gold, frankincense, and myrrh (Matthew 2:8-11).

The wise men are probably thinking, "Wow, God! You're so awesome. Not only do you lead us and guide us, but now this political leader is interested in worshiping the Christ as well. Not only will we find the greatest king the world has ever known, we will lead the king of Judea to worship at His throne."

The good news is that, if you are pure of heart, the Lord will protect you from the deceptions of the likes of Herod. God warns them in a dream not to go back to the palace. *"Then, being divinely warned in a dream that they should not return to Herod, they departed for their own country another way"* (Matt. 2:12). The Lord knows how to deliver you out of the hand of the political spirit, wherever it is operating.

As soon as the wise men were on their way, Joseph has a dream. The angel of the Lord instructs him to take his wife and baby to Egypt: *Behold, an angel of the Lord appeared to Joseph in a dream, saying, "Arise, take the young child and His mother, flee to Egypt, and stay there until I bring you word, for Herod will seek the young child to destroy Him"* (Matt. 2:13). Herod's true motive had been revealed.

Now what kind of a man is worried about being overthrown by a baby? A man motivated by a political spirit.

Here is the third characteristic of a political spirit: it is an invisible mastermind that wants to kill whatever God is doing at all costs. That is always at the heart of its hidden agenda. It seeks to make secret alliances to destroy the work of God. And so we read in Matthew 2:15 that Jesus was in Egypt *"until the death of Herod, that it might be fulfilled which was spoken by the Lord through the prophet, saying, 'Out of Egypt I called my son.' "*

Here is the third characteristic of a political spirit: it is an invisible mastermind that wants to kill whatever God is doing at all costs.

Sadly, the story doesn't end there. Herod finds out that the wise men didn't return because his motive was exposed. Remember, the Herodian spirit is about control, power, and reputation. If it feels that any of these are threatened, it will go to no end to protect and restore its position. Because he has failed to remove the infant king, Herod decrees that every single male child under the age of two must be put to death in the hopes that one of them will be this child. Thus there is a massacre of children in an attempt to eliminate the threat to Herod's throne (see Matt. 2:16-18).

So let me sum this up briefly: the political spirit is all about protecting position, power, and influence. It will use knowledge secretly and make secret alliances to preserve its personal kingdom against God's Kingdom. On the surface, it seems open, moral, and full of integrity, but it always has different motives than what it lets others see. And, because it always hides behind other spirits and a facade of friendship and trustworthiness, it is very difficult to perceive without a revelation from the Spirit of God. These are all important keys that will help you recognize the aims of this spirit and how it operates.

Dangerous Alliances

Let's go back to your life for a moment. Perhaps you have dealt with a religious spirit and didn't know about the strong man or political spirit operating behind it. You tried to get victory over a religious spirit when you needed, instead, to be binding the strong man that was operating behind it. Until you identify the political spirit that is in alliance with the religious spirit, you will be battling in vain. Two heads—or in this case, seven, as the Scriptures tell us (see Matt. 12:45)—will grow back for every one that you cut off. Whatever victory you achieve will only allow the strong man to return seven times stronger. The religious spirit will come back worse than before because you did not deal with the true source of your problems. When you begin to detect the political spirit, it will cunningly misdirect your attention toward the operation of the religious spirit and leave you battling it in never-ending cycles while it goes on about its business untouched.

The political spirit will also forge alliances behind the scenes with other spirits, such as the Jezebel spirit. Perhaps you have heard how the Jezebel spirit attempts to destroy prophets—or perverts the prophetic—by creating a prophetic counterfeit (see Rev. 2:20). Again, the only way to overcome the Jezebel spirit is to overcome the strong man or mastermind that is using it. The political spirit may even use both the Jezebel and religious spirits to ultimately forward its hidden agenda.

In Matthew chapter 14, we read about another Herod who makes an alliance with the Jezebel spirit. Remember that before Herod the Great died, he decided that his three sons would take power over different regions throughout Judea. The Herod we read about in Matthew 14 is called Herod Antipas and is ruling as a tetrarch, or governor, over the region of Galilee. This Herod seeks to kill the prophet, John the Baptist, and uses the Jezebel spirit to achieve it.

> *At that time Herod the tetrarch heard the report about Jesus and said to his servants, "This is John the Baptist; he is risen from the dead, and therefore these powers are at work in him." For Herod had laid hold of John and bound him, and put him in prison for the sake of Herodias, his brother Philip's wife. Because John had said to him, "It is not lawful for you to have her." And although he wanted to put him to death, he feared the multitude, because they counted him as a prophet* (Matthew 14:1-5).

The Herodian spirit in his heart wanted to kill John the Baptist because John had said it was unlawful for Herod Antipas to have his brother's wife. Herod seduces his niece, who was married to his brother Philip, and takes Herodias, which was her name, as his own wife.[2] So the prophet of the day, John the Baptist, comes out and says, "Hold on a minute! God's got a problem with this!" And the prophet speaks forth righteousness. So Herod wants to have him killed, but he can't do it outright because he fears public opinion, he fears *"the multitude because they counted him* [John] *as a prophet."*

Another characteristic of the political spirit is that it is concerned with what people think—it is occupied with reputation and public opinion.

Another characteristic of the political spirit is that it is concerned with what people think—it is occupied with reputation and public opinion. Does that sound like politics? From the time Jesus is born until the time He dies, this spirit is in operation. It smooth talked the Pharisees and flattered the wise men to get at Jesus while He was still a baby, and now it wants to kill John the Baptist. However, to get at John, this strong man will use another clandestine alliance to keep from compromising its position. In Matthew 14:6-10, we read about the political spirit's unique strategy to have John killed:

> *But when Herod's birthday was celebrated, the daughter of Herodias danced before them and pleased Herod. Therefore he promised with an oath to give her whatever she might ask.*
>
> *So she, having been prompted by her mother, said, "Give me John the Baptist's head here on a platter."*
>
> *And the king was sorry; nevertheless, because of the oaths and because of those who sat with him, he commanded it to be given to her. So he sent and had John beheaded in prison.*

Herodias was under the influence of the Jezebel spirit in this situation. The motive of the Jezebel spirit is to take out the prophet. So the strong man says to itself, "I need to remove this prophet. The best way to do that is to put Jezebel on assignment." So he finds a way to make a covenant—or an alliance—with her and kill the prophet. Herodias, which literally means "wife of Herod," has her daughter dance seductively, knowing it will please her husband. The Jezebel spirit is on assignment, believing that it is actually manipulating Herod in order to achieve its goal of destroying the prophet. Meanwhile, Herod, under the influence of the political spirit, is getting his way and accomplishing his desire. The deception and counter-deception is dizzying. So the daughter, *"prompted by her mother,"* asks for John the Baptist's head.

In the spirit realm, an alliance is created between the political spirit and the Jezebel spirit to remove a prophet. Most often we only look at the Jezebel spirit, reasoning that this was the spirit provoked by John the Baptist, which is true. But in this story we also see the strong man, whose real aim is to keep the government of God from being established, in operation behind the scenes.

It doesn't end here either because Herod also wants to kill Jesus. When the disciples tell Jesus of John's death, it says, *"He departed from there by boat to a deserted place by Himself"* (Matt. 14:13). Jesus did not want to stick around because He knew it wasn't the season for Him to deal with Herod. We know that Herod sought to kill Him because in Luke 9:9 we read, *"Herod said, 'John I have beheaded, but who is this of whom I hear such things?' So he sought to see Him."* Herod is thinking, "I have killed John the Baptist. Now who is this Jesus fellow? His reputation is growing, I better seek Him out and kill Him too." Do you see how this spirit operates?

Political Deception

Further on in the gospel of Luke we read how Jesus describes the political spirit after *"some Pharisees came, saying to Him,*

"Get out and depart from here, for Herod wants to kill You"
(Luke 13:31). Jesus responds to them in the next verse saying,
"Go, tell that fox, 'Behold, I cast out demons and perform cures
today and tomorrow, and the third day I shall be perfected' "
(Luke 13:32). Jesus refers to Herod as a "fox" because that is
another description of how the political spirit operates. A fox is a
cunning, crafty animal. If you look up the word *fox* in the
Merriam-Webster Dictionary you will find one of the meanings
is "a clever crafty person."[3]

Interestingly, one of the definitions of the adjective *politic* is
"crafty or cunning."[4] If we break this word down and look at the
Latin meaning of the prefix *poli,* we'll find it means "citizen."
The syllable *tic* in Latin is literally "silent" while the Greek version *tec* means "artful." The suffix *al* means "like."[5] Putting all of
that together, we might get "silent, artful-like citizen." We can see
how this relates to Herod and why the word *political* has come to
have the connotation that it has.

One man who is associated with political cunning is Niccolo
Machiavelli (1469-1527), who was a political leader and philoso-
pher who greatly influenced modern politics. The term
Machiavellian is defined as "using clever trickery, amoral methods, and expediency to achieve a desired goal, especially in politics."[6] It could be said that Herod possessed a *Machiavellian*
intelligence, an expression used in psychology for a type of
social intelligence "that involves the use of deception and the for-
mation of coalitions."[7]

In Luke chapter 12, Herod forms a sort of coalition with the
Pharisees and chief priests to threaten Jesus. Again, you see this

political leader, Herod of Antipas, enter into an alliance with the religious leadership. Have you ever been intimidated by a religious spirit working against you? You go to war with the religious spirit, not knowing that it is the strong man—this Herodian spirit—that is provoking the religious spirit to come against you. It is using deception by way of a coalition to throw you off.

Before I make these next few statements let me clarify that God does call people into political office and governmental positions of authority. He even calls Prophets and men and women of God to influence the very realm of government in nations that are secular or ungodly. We have great examples of such in the Bible like Daniel in Babylon and Joseph in Egypt. However, they did have to confront and overcame the strongman of their times in order to walk in their God-given assignment.

Having said that, far too often religious leaders have entered into political alliances with political parties thinking they are impacting the world only to find out they were actually prostituting their platforms of influence to forward hidden political agendas. Often political parties have come to religious leaders asking them to explain the Bible to them as if they were genuinely interested in the cause of Christ. What they are actually doing is using the Church to forward their agenda to get votes, rather than using their platform as a voice for righteousness, as they would have the religious community believe. The Church thinks it is impacting the political realm when really it is being used to forward political agendas. That is what Herod did with the Pharisees and tried to do with the wise men.

Often political parties have come to religious leaders asking them to explain the Bible to them as if they were genuinely interested in the cause of Christ.... The Church thinks it is impacting the political realm when really it is being used to forward political agendas.

This type of allegiance is going to hurt some ministries in the future. Ministries making allegiances with political agendas masquerading as a quest for the greater good may actually be yielding to the political spirit that intends to silence their voice through compromise and miss out on the original intent of their platform of influence. They will be measured according to the plumb line and found lacking. There is going to be trouble for them in the future because they are being used to forward ungodly political agendas that have nothing to do with establishing the true government and ways of God's Kingdom.

Yes, God wants to bring the Kingdom of God to the forefront. God wants His government to impact the world's government in every arena. But we don't need a false government in the political realm to give us credibility and to make us who God has said we already are. We need God's government to come so that we can be established in truth and righteousness, independent of any corrupting alliances.

This is the same trap that Judas fell into. Many think of Judas as a conniver and an obvious traitor, but he was in fact the most upstanding member of the disciples. Otherwise, why would they have trusted him as their treasurer? Even when Jesus told the disciples that there was a traitor among them, and then handed the sop of bread to Judas and told him to go do what he had to do, the disciples still looked back at Jesus and asked again who the betrayer was, even though He had just tried to point him out! (See John 13:26.)

Judas thought that Jesus had come to establish an earthly kingdom—that He would raise up an army, chase out the Romans, and then establish the Kingdom of God on the earth with Jesus, the son of David, as the new King of Israel. He expected that the chief priest and the Sanhedrin were going to bless Jesus and proclaim Him as the King of the Jews, an act that would start the revolution and end Roman rule. Instead, however, Judas was used by Caiaphas in the same way Herod had tried to use the wise men, except Caiaphas's scheme worked because Judas's motives were corrupt while the wise men's had been pure. Then, when Judas understood that he had been duped and had delivered Jesus to be crucified instead of proclaimed king, he couldn't live with himself and committed suicide, throwing their bribery money back in their faces (see Matt. 27:3-5). If only he had waited to see what God really had in store through His hidden wisdom and the power of the *spiritual* Kingdom that would be established as a result!

The political spirit will always try to buy, corrupt, or manipulate prophets in this manner to suit its hidden agenda.

The political spirit will always try to buy, corrupt, or manipulate prophets in this manner to suit its hidden agenda. It is a false honor for these religious leaders to be seen with crafty political leaders who aren't truly Christian but who want the vote of the Christian block. The political spirit is also trying to get a hold on what God is saying so that it can counteract God's will and the establishment of His Kingdom. Judas fell prey to an alliance of the political spirit and the religious spirit and became a pawn in the political spirit's quest to overthrow the work of Jesus. However, God's secret wisdom turned the crucifixion that followed into the greatest victory the Kingdom of God would ever experience.

The Herodian spirit has no loyalty whatsoever to anybody or anything. It does not stand for anything but its own self-interest. You cannot get this spirit in a room and figure out what its purpose or plan is. It will have a private meeting with you and enter into an alliance with you—its plan will be the same as yours and your plan will be the same as its. If someone is operating under this spirit, they will say they are with you one hundred percent. Then when they leave the room, they will enter into another alliance with someone else.

The Herodian spirit has no loyalty whatsoever to anybody or anything.

Note that such meetings and relationships are always kept private. They will never say anything about any of it in public. In fact, they never say much. They will let you do the talking. If they want to remove you, they will empower the Jezebel spirit or religious spirits around you to take you out. It is like the mafia lord who never gets his hands dirty.

But you, because you are trying to live for righteousness and to do what God has called you to do, are the one that has to deal with the strong man. You are the representative of God's government wherever God puts you. Whatever area, region, company, job, or ministry God has put you in, you are the person God has called to bind the strong man. On one hand, you have to deal with the Jezebel or religious spirits, and on the other you have to discern the political spirit that is in allegiance with them. This is not always obvious because the political spirit is cunning and will always appear to be on your side. It will flatter and promote you, but in truth, it is empowering the enemies of God's destined purpose for your life. In Mark 3:6, we are told how *"the proud religious law-keepers went out and made plans with the followers of King Herod how they might kill Jesus"* (NLV). Or, as it says in the English Standard Version, *"The Pharisees held counsel with the Herodians against Him, how to destroy Him."* This dangerous alliance is at work against the Christ in you today.

What was at the root of the Pharisees wanting to destroy Jesus? It was envy. The Pharisees were jealous of Jesus and that is why they sought to kill Him: *"...The chief priests had handed Him over because of envy"* (Mark 15:10). Envy is the primary vehicle that the political spirit uses to corrupt the hearts of leaders—and it is primarily what motivates the political spirit itself.

Envy is the primary vehicle that the political spirit uses to corrupt the hearts of leaders.

In Luke, we observe another characteristic of the Herodian, or political, spirit. After the Pharisees and the chief priests captured Jesus, when He was brought to Herod, we read: *When Herod saw Jesus, he was exceedingly glad; for he had desired for a long time to see Him, because he had heard many things about Him, and he hoped to see some miracle done by Him* (Luke 23:8). The political spirit behind Herod sought to mock Jesus—it is a mocking spirit. Don't forget that Herod wanted to kill Jesus all along. Remember, we read in Luke 13:31 that the Pharisees told Jesus, *"Herod wants to kill You."*

The political spirit is a mocking spirit.

So after Jesus is taken to Herod, *"He questioned Him with many words, but He answered him nothing. And the chief priests and scribes stood and vehemently accused Him"* (Luke 23:9-10). Notice that it is the religious spirit doing the accusing. *"Then Herod, with his men of war, treated Him with contempt and mocked Him, arrayed Him in a gorgeous robe, and sent Him back to Pilate"* (Luke 23:11). Herod wants Jesus dead, but notice how cunning he is. Herod does not want to be held responsible in the public eye, so he sends Him back to Pilate. As a result, Pilate and Herod become friends, though before they had been archenemies (see Luke 23:12). On account of their alliance, Pilate feels pressured to follow through with the execution of Jesus. Meanwhile, Pilate is convicted in his heart because his wife had a dream and warns him to be careful with how he handles Jesus. Herod's influence is more powerful than Pilate's conscience—and because of this new political alliance, Pilate is forced to forward Herod's agenda of putting Jesus to death.

> **Herod wants Jesus dead, but notice how cunning he is. Herod does not want to be held responsible in the public eye, so he sends Him back to Pilate.**

Expelling Darkness

For many years now, the western Church has been dealing with the religious spirit and the Jezebel spirit and can't figure out why it can never get complete victory over either. The reason is that we keep taking out the pawns but never get to the kingpin—the strong man. Thus the political spirit has gotten a foothold and has established legal access to and jurisdiction in the western Church. God wants to dismantle this demonic influence and replace it with the government of God's Kingdom so that His people can manifest and walk in the glory of the covenant. Thus the *kairos* time we are in: God is preparing a remnant that will have the jurisdictional authority to deal with this political spirit when light comes and its dark agenda is exposed.

When the Church gets a revelation of what is actually happening in the spirit realm, intercessory mantles will fall and a new wave of prophetic intercession will take place. Men and women of authority will arise because they will have diagnosed the true source of the symptoms that we have been fighting. They will have the knowledge and understanding necessary to take authority over it in prayer, as well as the wisdom to establish and maintain true government in their lives and in the Church once they do. They will put on the whole armor of God to then stand and stay standing without yielding.

Ephesians 6:11 tells you to *"put on the whole armor of God, that you may be able to stand against the wiles of the devil."* The enemy has deceitful strategies, but Ephesians 3:10 says that, *"through the church the manifold wisdom of God might now be made known to the rulers and authorities in the heavenly places"* (ESV). In other words, God's objective is that you and I would reveal the wisdom of God, which will expose and confound the principalities and powers working against us. We need understanding, and we need the deepest wisdom of God.

Meditation Points

- How would you describe the political spirit as we have looked at it so far? List its normal strategies and motives.

- What are the characteristics of this cunning entity?

- How does it make alliances?

- Have you ever encountered this spirit before, or do you know someone who has? Get them a copy of this book.

• Can you think of examples from current politics that reflect the work of the political spirit?

Endnotes

1. James Strong, LL.D., S.T.D. Universal Subject Guide to the Bible, 93. Richards Complete Bible Dictionary, 482-483. And Flavius Josephus, *The Jewish War*, translated by Robert Traill (London: Houlston & Stoneman, 1851).

2. http://www.jewishvirtuallibrary.org/jsource/History/herodian.html; accessed February 2008.

3. *Merriam-Webster Dictionary*, online, s.v. "Fox," http://www.merriam-webster.com/dictionary/fox; accessed 28 August 2008.

4. *The Free Dictionary*, s.v. "Politic," http://www.thefreedictionary.com/politic; accessed 28 August 2008.

5. "Greek and Latin Roots," *Kent School District*, http://www.kent.k12.wa.us/ksd/MA/resources/greek_and_latin_roots/transition.html; accessed 28 August 2008.

6. *Encarta® World English Dictionary*, s.v. "Machiavellian," http://encarta.msn.com/dictionary_1861627559/Machiavellian.html; accessed 28 August 2008.

7. *Ibid.*, "Machiavellian intelligence," http://encarta.msn.com/dictionary_/Machiavellian%2520intelligence.html; accessed 28 August 2008.

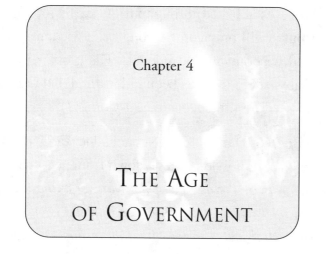

Chapter 4

THE AGE
OF GOVERNMENT

This decision is by the decree of the
watchers, And the sentence by the word
of the holy ones, In order that the living
may know That the Most High rules in
the kingdom of men (Daniel 4:17).

We are moving into an era when God's Kingdom is going to be manifested on a larger scale than the world has ever seen. It is a time when believers will act to institutionalize the Kingdom of God into our governmental systems. The Church is being called to come together to establish God's government—His ways, justice, and righteousness spread to all through His love. It is time for the Church to provide solutions to the world we live in. The world is looking for answers. God's people have an opportunity to disseminate the wisdom of God in order to resolve conflict by bringing divine justice to bear. God desires

His rule to be established throughout the earth for the good of humanity, but it will only come through His wisdom—for where the manifold wisdom of God prevails, His glory will be manifested. It is a wisdom that has been hidden and that God destined for our glory before time began (see 1 Cor. 2:7).

In the Book of Daniel, King Nebuchadnezzar had a dream in which a watcher, or holy one, came down from heaven crying out, *"This decision is by the decree of the watchers, and the sentence by the word of the holy ones, in order that the living may know that the Most High rules in the kingdom of men..."* (Dan. 4:17). We are moving into an age where this type of rule is coming— God's holy nation will be established upon the earth in principle and in practice. God's sovereign rule will bring hope and healing to humankind. God's government is a place where His will is unimpeded and His goodness flows to all without corruption. However, if the Church is not prepared, we will miss out on our role in this rule, as well as many of the benefits.

Of course, we know that God's will toward all is good. God is love. When it comes to us individually, how much does He love us? He loves each of us as if we were His favorite child. Don't you feel like you are His only child when you experience God's love for you? It is a love with which God desires to touch every life on the face of the planet. This is God's individual visitation to each individual believer—the Kingdom of God that He births within each and every one of His beloved children (see Luke 17:21).

> **There is also a corporate manifestation of God's love, and that is what the government of God is all about. It is to bring justice based on the corporate heart of love for all people equally.**

On the other hand, there is also a corporate manifestation of God's love, and that is what the government of God is all about. It is to bring justice based on the corporate heart of love for all people equally. That is what King Solomon did when two women were fighting over a baby, both claiming to be the mother. Solomon disseminated the wisdom of God and suggested cutting the baby in half and dividing it between the two women. Through this wisdom, he revealed who the real mother was and exposed the false. The real mother was willing to forfeit her rights to preserve the baby's life, while the false woman was willing to see the baby cut in half out of bitterness because she had already lost her own. Then Solomon was able to give the baby to the real mother (1 Kings 3:27).

This is why God calls people into certain areas of leadership: so they can represent the government of God's Kingdom by bringing solutions that reveal God's love equally for all people in every given situation. God's plan is that this will reach beyond the Church into a world looking for answers. It is God's ways and God's government being institutionalized into the governments of men. It is a government that brings God's love to bear on all people corporately. Simply put, it is God's will being done on the earth, and it is His original intent concerning the Church and the

Kingdom of God being released into the lives of every human being, believer and non-believer alike. It is His government functioning on earth as it does in Heaven.

Imagine for a moment what it would be like if God's will for you was readily available not only through the power of God, but also through human institutions. Let's take, for example, the issue of dealing with poverty and hunger. It is certainly not God's will that children die of hunger or live in squalor. Now on one level, God could individually touch their lives and give the parents favor for a better job and a better standard of living, but on another level, the Church as a Body could touch those people's lives to educate them and enable them to build a better life. The Church could do this in a way that does not take away people's dignity through a degrading welfare system, but that builds them up and enables them to go to the next level—a level that can sustain them. This is an example of God's love touching people through His fingers—members of the Church—acting corporately to bring about God's will for people on the earth. God invests His power in His Body, and then the individual parts of His Body work corporately to transform their surroundings. It is not a legalism that forces morality onto others, but it is God's love being institutionalized so that everyone is blessed.

God invests His power in His Body, and then the individual parts of His Body work corporately to transform their surroundings. It is not a legalism that forces morality onto others, but it is God's love being institutionalized so that everyone is blessed.

What if that happened with regard to healthcare, or education, or commerce and business? The establishment of God's government would literally be the institutionalization of Heaven on earth.

Let me give you a counter-example. If I go to Saudi Arabia, which is a Muslim country with a Muslim government, I can personally walk under an umbrella of God's covenant and blessing and protection if God has sent me there, even though the Saudi government is against me as a Christian minister. The government opposes me ministering and preaching the Gospel, even though I may be acting on specific instructions from the Lord. But if Saudi Arabia's government switched over and became a government backed by Christ Jesus, then I wouldn't need to operate under a special umbrella of God's divine protection. Then the government of the Kingdom of God would begin to manifest, and I would have freedom to walk in the fullness of God's calling as a minister and evangelist. However, since Saudi Arabia is an Islamic government today, I do not have that level of freedom to preach the Gospel there yet.

I live in Canada, though, and despite the fact that our government is secular, the Gospel is not forbidden. I can openly preach Jesus in the streets and on television. I am not censored. Because Christians have stood for what is right in our country since its foundations, we have freedom of religion.

Governments set the boundaries for what can and cannot be done within their jurisdiction. Usually, but not always, they impose laws that are for the good of society. Ideally, legal limitations are a manifestation of the good intentions of the government toward its people.

To establish God's government would be to institutionalize His good will toward all people. As the angels said at Christ's coming, *"Glory to God in the highest, and on earth peace, good will toward men"* (Luke 2:14). The first part of establishing this Kingdom happened when salvation was made available to all through Jesus. His will is that none should perish but that all would come to everlasting life (John 3:16). Jesus died for *all* mankind. He died for the sins of the *whole* world. Even if people don't know about Him, God still loves them and wants to save them. Does Jesus love you and me as much as He loves the wicked sinner? Absolutely. He loves us all equally and specifically. In God's governmental heart, there is a love for everybody. God's corporate love is about being fair and just. The government of God is God's way of bringing justice, and this, at times, will also bring judgment. When we operate under God's government, it is His justice that protects us—and His judgment that disciplines and prepares us to live better, more fruitful lives.

We read in First Peter 4:17 that *"the time has come for judgment to begin at the house of God...."* For sons and daughters of God, judgment is nothing to be afraid of. It is actually good news. The word *judgment* is *krema* in the Greek, which means "an opportunity for you to make a decision."[1] Thus judgment is an opportunity in our lives when God gives us choices. It is a time of preparation and testing—of refinement and discovering the true nature of our hearts. We are in such a season right now. God wants us to be able to discern the season, to know what He is doing, and to shift into it appropriately.

We must embrace the current season of preparation before the unrolling of His government. He has been waiting. He has been preparing us. He wants us to take our positions of authority and to become postured to bless. He must put all of His pieces and people into place before He can release His glory upon the earth in a measure greater than it has been seen since creation.

More Leaven

In Acts 12, we gain more insight into the operation of the Herodian spirit against the early Church. We have already looked at what was taking place during the time when the first Herod came to power. The political spirit worked through Herod the Great to try to kill Jesus while He was still in the manger. The political spirit later worked through his son, Herod Antipas, to prevent Jesus from fulfilling His divine mandate by first beheading His prophet, John the Baptist, and then by sending Christ to be crucified via an alliance with Pontius Pilate. So, in Acts 12, we see the political spirit attempting to dismantle the early Church through Herod Agrippa, the grandson of Herod the Great.

King Agrippa I was the king in power when the apostles began expanding the ranks of believers and establishing the Church. This is what we read about him in the opening of Acts 12:

> Now about that time Herod the king stretched out his hand to harass some from the church. Then he killed James the brother of John with the sword. And because he saw that it pleased the Jews, he proceeded further to seize Peter also... (Acts 12:1-3).

As the glory of God moves out, the Herodian spirit moves in. The apostles are going forth and expanding God's Kingdom. The Word of God is being multiplied so that already thousands have come to the knowledge of Christ. People are giving their finances, property, whatever they have to support the work of the ministry (see Acts 4:37).

In the wake of God Himself coming to dwell among and minister to people, God now dwells within and is working through them. Herod retaliates with a vengeance.

A great move of God is taking place through the prayers and zeal of new believers. Throughout this season, God's Word is being preached with power—signs and wonders following—and the Church is growing in knowledge and faith. God's Kingdom is on the move. Something is about to happen that the world has never witnessed. In the wake of God Himself coming to dwell among and minister to people, God now dwells within and is working through them. Herod retaliates with a vengeance. He seeks to regain control of the people's hearts and minds. So he kills James, and when he observes that it pleases the Jews to kill James, he seeks to kill Peter also. And to make the greatest impact, he intends to bring Peter before the people immediately following Passover.

> *...Now it was during the Days of Unleavened Bread. So when he had arrested him, he put him in prison, and delivered him to four squads of soldiers to keep him, intending to bring him before the people after Passover* (Acts 12:3-4).

That is the way this spirit works. However, in this instance, the Church springs into action and with fervent unity begins praying for Peter to be delivered. Their voices are heard on high, and just as Herod is about to have Peter brought out, an angel appears to liberate him. When Peter is safely away, he says aloud, *"Now I know for certain that the Lord has...delivered me from the hand of Herod and from all the expectation of the Jewish people"* (Acts 12:11). Herod may not have succeeded in killing Peter, but he manages to manipulate public opinion in his favor. His media blitz has them both intimidated and impressed. Listen to what he does in Acts 12:21-22: *"On a set day Herod, arrayed in royal apparel, sat on his throne and gave an oration to them. And the people kept shouting, 'The voice of a god and not of a man!'"* Herod basks in the adoration of the people. But the hand of God is in operation, and this is what happens next: *"Then immediately an angel of the Lord struck him, because he did not give glory to God. And he was eaten by worms and died"* (Acts 12:23).

King Herod attempted to forego God's ways and to establish his own. Why was the hand of God operating to such a degree during this time? Because God's government was being established in the earth through the entrance of the Word made flesh in the person of Jesus and then in the foundations being laid by the Apostles and Prophets around the chief cornerstone Jesus Christ. The kingdom was being established within the Body of Christ ready to be released to change the world around them. This is why the political spirit was so active through Herod and his descendants. As we saw in Chapter 3, the seed of Esau was responding to the rise of the seed of Jacob.

Once the strong man (acting through Herod) is displaced by the hand of the Lord, *"The word of God grew and multiplied"* (Acts 12:24). It is not a coincidence that Herod dies just before this takes place. It is in the next chapter of Acts that you see the commissioning of Saul and Barnabas into a governmental apostolic assignment. They were always called to be apostles, but they are not separated and sent out by the Holy Spirit (see Acts 13:2). God was about to do something extraordinary. He was positioning His Church in strategic places throughout the ancient world. One of the first locations was Antioch in Syria, the most important city in the Near East, second only to Alexandria. Antioch was the first place that believers were called Christians and that faith in Jesus Christ was recognized as something more than another Jewish sect.

The political spirit will always surface just before true government comes.

The government of God was being established on the heels of Herod's death. The political spirit will always surface just before true government comes. When deceptive power is removed, it must be replaced with divine power—and that is what we see happening as the apostles move in to establish God's authority. We talked about the strong man in Matthew 12 and about Jesus' teaching that you cannot take a kingdom, city, or house unless you first bind the strong man—only then can you claim that territory and replace it with Jesus Christ's lordship and authority. This is how an apostle thinks. When an apostle is sent into an area, he is thinking about how to seize territory and put it under the lordship and dominion of the government of Jesus Christ—God's chief apostle.

When we talk about apostolic government and authority, there are no options, no arguments, and no discussions with the enemy. The apostle puts a stake in the ground and hangs a flag on it. You may not see it, but this flag represents the Kingdom of God and the reality that Jesus Christ is lord over that area. From that point forward, powers and principalities know that the government of Jesus Christ is in operation. This is what Paul and Barnabas were commissioned by God to do as apostles. This is why Herod Agrippa's son, King Agrippa II, opposed them. However, by the time Agrippa II sent Paul to Rome, where he was martyred, the fire of God's glory was already ablaze—His government had already been set in motion. When King Agrippa II died in A.D. 92, the Herodian dynasty ended, but the Church had only just begun to rise.

The Hand of the Lord

In the New Testament, we also see more effects of the hand of the Lord when the government of God is not honored. In Acts 5, we read about a move of God that takes place under Peter's ministry. Believers come and lay their possessions at the apostles' feet. It begins when a wealthy man named Barnabas sells all of his possessions for the purpose of spreading the Gospel and taking care of the poor. A man and his wife, Ananias and Sapphira, find themselves in the midst of this holy move of the Spirit. They take lightly something that is very holy; they give into the temptation to do things their own way rather than God's way. When they sell their land and bring the proceeds to Peter, they secretly withhold some of the profit to spend on themselves, but they tell the Church that they have given it all in order to be honored among them. Peter discerns their impure motives and calls Ananias to task:

> *"Ananias, why has Satan filled your heart to lie to the Holy Spirit and keep back part of the price of the land for yourself? While it remained, was it not your own? And after it was sold, was it not in your own control? Why have you conceived this thing in your heart? You have not lied to men but to God." Then Ananias, hearing these words, fell down and breathed his last...* (Acts 5:3-5).

Can you imagine that happening in church today? You would have to train your ushers to carry out the lifeless bodies of those who did not give with a pure heart. *"And the young men arose and wrapped him up, carried him out, and buried him"* (Acts 5:6). This happened in the New Testament—it is what happens when God's government is in place.

You might say, "Well, I've heard of people who have vowed to the Lord and made a pledge and didn't do what they said they would do. How come they are still alive?" This is not a formula. This has nothing to do with legalism. We live in an age of grace, but also an age with a limited presence of God's glory. That moment in Church history was a sovereign move of God, and people were coming and laying everything they had at the apostles' feet. They are acting in one accord with singleness of heart when Ananias enters their midst with his heart out of line with God's sovereign government. God is a discerner of the thoughts and intents of the heart (see Heb. 4:12). Ananias touches a holy, sacred thing that God is doing in their hearts. That is why judgment comes and he dies prematurely.

About three hours later, when his wife comes in, Peter gives her an opportunity to speak the truth, but she gives the same story as her husband, and she meets the same fate:

Then Peter said to her, "How is it that you have agreed together to test the Spirit of the Lord? Look, the feet of those who have buried your husband are at the door, and they will carry you out." Then immediately she fell down at his feet and breathed her last. And the young men came in and found her dead, and carrying her out, buried her by her husband. So great fear came upon all the church and upon all who heard these things (Acts 5:9-11).

Whenever God's divine government operates, there will be an equal evidence of His love for all people, which is the fruit of the fear of the Lord.

And what was the result? *"Great fear came upon all the church and upon all who heard these things."* Whenever God's divine government operates, there will be an equal evidence of His love for all people, which is the fruit of the fear of the Lord. The fear of the Lord brings His authority to bear. The fear of the Lord is the gateway to His wisdom.

In the very next verses we read, *"And through the hands of the apostles many signs and wonders were done among the*

people...And believers were increasingly added to the Lord, mul-
titudes of both men and women" (Acts 5:12,14). Believers are
increasingly added to the Lord. There is the fruit of His love.

Something so holy is taking place that it cannot be violated.
The anointing and power that God gave to Peter was according to
the governmental call. A judgment takes place right away. It is,
however, a judgment that is for the benefit of all the people,
because the fear of the Lord had to come and believers had to be
added. He couldn't allow this thing to enter in and destroy the
move of God. In essence, it was a safeguard for everyone, but it
was also the sovereignty and glory of God in action.

Looking at Acts 13 again, we see another example of divine
order being established in the early Church. As we saw before,
Barnabas and Paul are separated out by the Holy Spirit to do the
work for which God had called them. They are sent out with an
apostolic anointing and authority. One of their first missions is to
Cyprus, where Barnabas hailed from. There the proconsul hears
of what they were preaching and wants to meet with them *"to*
hear the word of God" (Acts 13:7).

The proconsul was the highest governing authority in the
region. He was the Roman Emperor's top representative on the
island of Cyprus. But a false prophet has sought the proconsul's
favor and has been consulting with him. When he hears of his
desire to meet with Paul and Barnabas, because of his own inter-
est in making an alliance with this political leader, the *"sor-*
cerer...withstood them, seeking to turn the proconsul away from
the faith" (Acts 13:8). We read what happens as a result in the
next verses:

Then Saul, who also is called Paul, filled with the Holy Spirit, looked intently at him and said, "O full of all deceit and all fraud, you son of the devil, you enemy of all righteousness, will you not cease perverting the straight ways of the Lord? And now, indeed, the hand of the Lord is upon you, and you shall be blind, not seeing the sun for a time." And immediately a dark mist fell on him, and he went around seeking someone to lead him by the hand (Acts 13:9-11).

The hand of the Lord comes upon this man and strikes him blind. The government of God is in operation, exposing the false and revealing the truth. *"Then the proconsul believed, when he saw what had been done, being astonished at the teaching of the Lord"* (Acts 13:12). Something happens when the Sovereign Lord commissions Paul. The hand of the Lord comes upon Paul for his apostolic ministry, and he is sent into this territory to do a work for God. It had nothing to do with Paul as a person. He did not come up with this idea on his own. He was there to establish God's divine authority, government, and sovereign rule, and when someone interfered, they came up against the hand of the Lord. When God's government comes, this type of power operates freely.

When this type of governmental authority came upon the apostles, signs and wonders followed them. Mighty deeds were done.

When this type of governmental authority came upon the apostles, signs and wonders followed them. Mighty deeds were done. With great power they were bearing witness to the resurrection of Jesus. Heaven backed them up. The hand of the Lord was upon them, backing them up on behalf of God's government. When you act on behalf of God's government, God will back you up too.

Divine Justice

In the Old Testament, we also read about kings and priests who attempt to set up their own governing systems. These patterns are recorded for us so that we can begin to discern the works of this "politicizing" tactic of the enemy. Though they were priests and representatives of God, they subtly opposed God's rule and sought to operate according to their own rules. King Solomon falls prey to this toward the end of his life by marrying women who worship false gods. Solomon allows them to bring their idols into his home and to continue worshiping them under his watch. As a result, God tells Solomon that He will remove the kingdom from his heirs and give it over to one of his servants. After King Solomon dies, there is a dispute about taxes in Israel so that the ten northern tribes are separated and come under the kingship of Solomon's former servant, Jeroboam. God's nation on the earth, Israel, set up by the godly David, lasts less than two generations before it is divided because of Solomon's compromise (1 Kings 11:31).

God says to Solomon that He will not give the whole kingdom over to Jeroboam, however. He will hold a little back for David's descendants, for David's sake. But the ten northern tribes come under the rule and kingship of Jeroboam (1 Kings 11:35). This is where we begin to clearly see false government take hold in Israel. It was a first step away from God's government and ways.

Not long after Jeroboam became king, he notices that, because the temple was in Jerusalem, all the tribes of Israel have to go to Judah at least three times a year to celebrate the many feasts. As a result, Jeroboam thinks that he is losing popularity and fears that he will lose control. So he issues a decree that the ten tribes no longer have to go to Jerusalem. Instead, they can celebrate the feasts in the northern town of Bethel (1 Kings 12:32). Another step away from God's government is taken.

By operating politically rather than righteously, he creates a false order of priesthood so that he can keep the people under his power. That is the intention and motive of his heart.

In order to fulfill his plan, Jeroboam appoints his own priests. In so doing, he has not only established a false government, he is also establishing a false religion. By operating politically rather than righteously, he creates a false order of priesthood so that he can keep the people under his power. That is the intention and motive of his heart.

In First Kings 13, we read about a young prophet who goes to the altar of Bethel where Jeroboam is burning incense. The young prophet walks up to Jeroboam and prophesies over the altar.

And behold, a man of God went from Judah to Bethel by the word of the Lord, and Jeroboam stood by the altar to burn incense. Then he cried out against the altar by the word of the Lord, and said, "O altar, altar! Thus says the Lord: 'Behold, a child, Josiah by name, shall be born to the house of David; and on you he shall sacrifice the priests of the high places who burn incense on you, and men's bones shall be burned on you'" (1 Kings 13:1-2).

He goes on to prophesy, *"This is the sign which the Lord has spoken: Surely the altar shall split apart, and the ashes on it shall be poured out"* (1 Kings 13:3). In the next verse you read, *When King Jeroboam heard the saying of the man of God, who cried out against the altar in Bethel, that he stretched out his hand from the altar, saying, "Arrest him!" Then his hand, which he stretched out toward him, withered, so that he could not pull it back to himself* (1 Kings 13:4).

Jeroboam has been running things according to the strategies of the political spirit for a while. He doesn't realize that a prophet has come who is carrying God's authority. This young prophet represents a higher government than the false government Jeroboam had set up. So what happens next? *"The altar also was split apart, and the ashes poured out from the altar, according to the sign which the man of God had given by the word of the Lord"* (1 Kings 13:5). When the king sees this, he says to the man of God, *"Please entreat the favor of the Lord your God, and pray for me, that my hand may be restored to me"* (1 Kings 13:6). The prophet does entreat the Lord on the king's behalf, and God shows mercy and heals his hand.

Years later, the rest of this prophecy is fulfilled. Josiah overthrows Jeroboam's temple and some of the priests who are killed were the ones Jeroboam had ordained. Josiah overturns the false

order of priesthood and government and restored a righteous one
(2 Kings 23:15-25).

Governmental Authority for This Season

We are moving into an era when we will see the government
of God in the western world. There have been men and women in
this century who have operated with this type of governmental
authority. One such person was a man by the name of Benson
Idahosa (1938-1998) who evangelized a large portion of Africa.
It was known in his meetings that if anyone spoke against him,
like the false prophet did against Paul, they would suffer severe
physical trauma. Many would die in his meetings if they did not
repent. He had an authority from Heaven. The Kingdom of God
had jurisdiction wherever he walked. It may be hard to believe,
but as we have seen, this was not unusual in the early Church.

If we talk about a New Testament-patterned Church and if we
want the miracles, signs, wonders, and glory, then we must be
prepared to deal with the ushers that have to handle those stricken
blind—or struck dead. If we truly want to have a revival of the
move of God as we saw it in the early Church, we cannot leave
out this aspect. If we want to see the hand of the Lord move
through the Church today, we must remember that it is as severe
as it is forgiving. God's love brings both justice and mercy.

God wants to prepare His people to receive His sovereign
rule in their personal and corporate lives. The purpose of God's
government, for the most part, is corporate. Similarly, though a
prophet may bring a word to someone individually, the purpose
of the prophet is to bring direction and correction to the people
of God as a whole. The prophet brings insight about seasons. His

primary purpose is not to speak to you individually. His primary purpose is to speak corporately to the people or the region that he is called to or to those in places of influence concerning God's eternal and corporate purposes in the earth.

> **The minute you are correctly positioned, the hand of the Lord will come on you. Now you are operating in conjunction with what God is doing in the present season. That is why it is important to be aware of what the prophets are saying.**

As an individual, the Holy Spirit is leading you. God is trying to get you under His hand to get you in a position of authority and blessing. The minute you are correctly positioned, the hand of the Lord will come on you. Now you are operating in conjunction with what God is doing in the present season. That is why it is important to be aware of what the prophets are saying. If a true prophet comes, he or she will tell you where the hand of the Lord is at work in this season. It used to be over there, but now it is over here—it used be working on that floor of the building, but now it is working on the next floor in this next season. God is continually building His temple and advancing His Kingdom.

As His Kingdom advances, there will be a clashing of the systems of man and the government of God. In this new era of government, we will witness massive conflicts. There will be a crumbling of man's systems, and the Jeroboams of our day are going to face an encounter with the sovereign hand of God. This is the season that we are moving into. The divine government of God is coming. This is good news!

We must do away with the mentality of "my ministry" and "my success." What is coming is an age of governmental authority—and that authority belongs to the King. It is His government; we are merely representatives.

When I am acting on behalf of a certain government, and the country I am sent to by that government refuses to listen to the message I am delivering, it is not my job to make them listen. If I go as an ambassador to a nation, I may say to another country's officials, "I have a message for you. If you don't stop terrorizing our people and destroying our embassies, my government will retaliate." If they don't listen, do I as an ambassador pull out my M-16? Of course not! I would simply back away from the table, board my government jet, and return to headquarters. This is the way of God—the other is the way of the political spirit.

In our personal lives, however, too many of us are used to pulling out the guns instead of leaving things to the hand of God. We are used to dealing with the enemy in our daily battles. We have been taught to take authority over the enemy and fight whatever comes against us. But this is a previous revelation of an old season having to do with personal authority. When you step into an assignment representing God's government, you can't take it upon yourself to get into skirmishes with the enemy. You must simply deliver the message that you have been given and let the Spirit of God take care of the rest. You have to learn to give place to the wrath of God by moving your personal self out of the way to make way for His government to respond.

In the same respect, it is not up to you and me to pass judgment on others. We read in Romans 14:4, *"Who are you to judge another's servant? To his own master he stands or falls...."* Never judge those who are in leadership or authority. If something is wrong, God says that He has a government that will deal with that issue. Again, in Romans we read, *"Let every soul be subject to the governing authorities. For there is no authority except from God, and the authorities that exist are appointed by God"* (Rom. 13:1). If you resist those in authority, you resist God. As we have seen, when you resist God, you bring judgment upon yourself.

When you know you are acting as an appointed representative of God, you can be confident that God will back you up in return. Once you get that in your heart, you will realize that you do indeed have a divinely ordained assignment and that all of Heaven is behind you.

On the other hand, when you know you are acting as an appointed representative of God, you can be confident that God will back you up in return. Once you get that in your heart, you will realize that you do indeed have a divinely ordained assignment and that all of Heaven is behind you. You will have supernatural boldness as you walk in the authority of Heaven. Will people oppose you? Absolutely! Your call wouldn't be true if they didn't. That is part of the assignment.

So, is what you are doing right now in your life on your own behalf? Did you call yourself? Are you a "went" rather than a "sent?" A "went" is someone who goes out on his or her own behalf. A "sent" is someone who goes out on behalf of the sender. When others receive you, whom do they receive? They receive Him that sent you. It is about the sender. Are they receiving you or God? That is the whole concept of divine purpose and assignment. It has nothing to do with you personally—it has everything to do with who you are representing.

The season we are moving into is one of divine assignments and missions. The false will soon be obvious as the glory of God is again released in His Body in a greater measure. I am here to prepare you, because manmade false governments—even in the Church, in North America, and in the western world—are going to fall and crumble in this next age. There cannot just be a displacement; there has to be a replacement and an establishment of godly order and government.

Testing the Spirits

As I have talked to people about the political spirit, they have asked how to deal with it. They ask, "Should we just pray about it?" That is a good start, but that is not enough. If you just pray about it and are not willing to change in order to align with God's government and order, this thing will go out and come back seven times stronger, and you will be worse off than you were before. The primary reason that God is establishing His government is to expose the false governing system that the political spirit works through and to empower us to overcome it.

A new era of divine order and authority will test the hearts and allegiance of God's people—*"The hour is coming, and now is, when the true worshipers will worship the Father in spirit and truth..."* (John 4:23). Keep your heart with all diligence because you will see the hand of the Lord at work in the Church. This era will usher in the glory of His presence. When the government of God comes, the glory will also come to reveal His majesty. This is the eternal purpose of your assignment. You are on earth because of your divine assignment—and if you are still here, then your assignment is not over.

The heart of God's government is key to understanding how God operates.

The Heart of Leadership God Is Seeking

The heart of God's government is key to understanding how God operates. Nowhere is this better illustrated than in Second Chronicles, where Solomon prays for wisdom. In Second Chronicles 1:6, the newly crowned Solomon makes a thousand offerings and sacrifices to the Lord. His father, the great King David, has just died. Solomon entreats God, "Like you were with my father David, would you be with me?" Something is revealed about Solomon's heart that we must understand—it compels God to appear to him inquiring, "Solomon, what do you want?" This is when Solomon asks for wisdom. In Hebrew, one of the meanings of the word *wisdom* is "a hearing and understanding heart."[2]

But even before Solomon makes his request, something about Solomon's heart moves God to appear before him. *"On that night God appeared to Solomon, and said to him, 'Ask! What shall I give you?' "* (2 Chron. 1:7). This was Solomon's reply:

> *You have shown great mercy to David my father, and have made me king in his place. Now, O Lord God, let Your promise to David my father be established, for You have made me king over a people like the dust of the earth in multitude.* **Now give me wisdom and knowledge, that I may go out and come in before this people; for who can judge this great people of Yours** (2 Chronicles 1:8-10).

Whose people is Solomon praying on behalf of? His people? The people of Israel? No, Solomon prays on behalf of the *people of God*. This is the key: in this leader's heart, he is acting on behalf of *God's* people, not his people. Watch God's response:

> *Then God said to Solomon: "Because this was in your heart, and you have not asked riches or wealth or honor or the life of your enemies, nor have you asked long life—but have asked wisdom and knowledge for yourself,* **that you may judge My people over whom I have made you king"** (2 Chronicles 1:11).

Usually when we hear the story of Solomon, we think, "Yes, he asked for wisdom." You have probably said to yourself, "If I ever have an encounter with the Lord, and He asks me that question, I'll answer, 'I want wisdom!' " But it isn't about what Solomon wants for himself, it is about his desire for the people of God. He wants to rule and judge righteously as a king, to represent God's government to God's people. This is his heart's motivation. He desires God's wisdom and knowledge so that he can act as a mediator between God and His people—*"that I may go out and come in before this people."*

This pleases God so much that He says, "Solomon, I'll give you everything. I'll even put you at peace with your enemies. Your father David had to fight. I'll not only give you what David had, but I'll give you one better. No more wars" (see 2 Chron. 1:12). So Solomon reigns over a period of unprecedented peace and prosperity. Unfortunately, later in his life, he becomes complacent and compromises—he acts on behalf of himself rather than the people of God—and in the end he has to fight the Edomites (1 Kings 11:14). However, while God's government is in operation, there is peace.

Peace is one of the byproducts of divine government.

Peace is one of the byproducts of divine government. The prophet Isaiah tells us that *"Of the increase of His government and peace there will be no end..."* (Isa. 9:7). Upon Christ's shoulders, the government will rest, and there will be peace. If God is enthroned in your home, you will have peace in your home, even while there is turmoil in society. That is why, during the millennial reign of Christ, when the Lord takes His throne in the earth, there will be peace. This is not only a personal peace; this is a corporate peace, which represents the divine order of God's government. The Bible also says to let the peace of God rule in our hearts (see Col. 3:15).That only begins when you start to reverence and honor the living God. When you begin to see the signs of God's sovereign move in your personal life, you are getting close to divine purpose.

God brings government, justice, and righteousness. "For the kingdom of God is…righteousness and peace and joy in the Holy Spirit" (Rom. 14:17). Where there is righteousness and peace, there is the government of God. And as surely as the knowledge of the glory of the Lord will fill the earth as the waters cover the sea (see Hab. 2:14), so will God establish His sovereign rule. *"Then the Lord said… 'Truly, as I live, all the earth shall be filled with the glory of the Lord' "* (Num. 14:20-21).

God brings government, justice, and righteousness.

In Proverbs 21:1, we read, *"The king's heart is in the hand of the Lord, like the rivers of water; He turns it wherever He wishes."* God can turn the heart of a king any direction He wants. We are asked to pray for those in authority because God wants us to let *Him* deal with those in authority. If you can embrace this truth and pray for those in authority over you, you will take a step toward allowing God to bring *you* into a place of divine authority. When He does, remember that God has not positioned you there as a result of your personal agenda but according to His corporate plan. You are there because your appointed time of assignment has come.

Taking your Position

These are things you need to know concerning the place we are going in the next season. The foundation of God's government is being laid. Flawed foundations will be broken up as fallow ground. Whatever is counterfeit will be removed. A new government will begin to manifest. God is raising up a people who will exercise His governmental authority—a people with the purest, most noble hearts. This is why we have been brought through these seasons of alignment and character testing. God does not want His authority abused. As representatives of God's government, we will truly reign as kings and priests in these last days.

Now your life makes sense. What you have been through is about your assignment. Your assignment is about godly government. What are you going to do with this new knowledge?

Meditation Points

- What would your workplace look like if the will of God flowed freely there? How would it change the way business was done? How would it affect your city and county governments? Your nation?

- Search the Scriptures for guidelines on how things should be done in a nation influenced by the government of the Kingdom.

- What can you do to release the Kingdom of God within you?

- What would you think if the hand of the Lord began striking down those who were lying to the Holy Spirit and the Church? How would things change? How does this kind of fear of God open doors to the deeper wisdom of God?

- What do you need to do to align yourself with God's government where you work, worship, and live?

- Will you embrace the heart of leadership that God is calling you to?

- How can the Kingdom within you change the culture around you?

- Are you ready to enter the age of government?

Endnotes

1. James Strong, S.T.D. LL.D., GREEK DICTIONARY OF THE NEW TESTAMENT (page 273). "Krema."

2. http://findarticles.com/p/articles/mi_qa3942/is_/ai_n9230736 (Lutheran, The, Feb 2003 by Farrington, Debra K) "Wisdom."

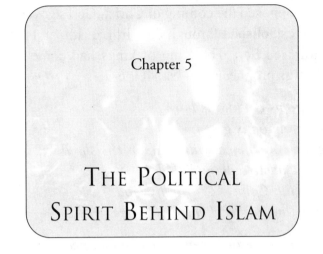

Chapter 5

THE POLITICAL
SPIRIT BEHIND ISLAM

*So Esau hated Jacob because of the blessing
with which his father blessed him, and Esau
said in his heart, "The days of mourning
for my father are at hand; then I will kill
my brother Jacob* (Genesis 27:41).

Another key to understanding the political spirit is to understand its history. I have given you some examples in terms of how
it operates, what its motives are, and how to identify it. It is the
strong man that opposes the work of Christ in the earth. It is the
darkness that the light of Christ has come forth to expose—the
gross darkness that only the glory of God can overcome. It is the
false and deceptive governing system that sets itself up against
the true government of God. It normally becomes most evident
when God's divine order is about to be established.

The strong man flexed his muscles through the reign of
Herod—it was embodied in the Herodian Dynasty, which

desperately opposed the coming of Christ. God's government was about to be established through the birth, death, and resurrection of the promised Son. The King of kings had come to take His throne, as was prophesied in Isaiah 9:6-7:

For unto us a Child is born,
Unto us a Son is given;
And the government will be upon His shoulder.
And His name will be called
Wonderful, Counselor, Mighty God,
Everlasting Father, Prince of Peace.

Of the increase of His government and peace
There will be no end,
Upon the throne of David and over His kingdom,
To order it and establish it with judgment and justice
From that time forward, even forever....

This is why we saw the political spirit manifested so powerfully through King Herod during the time of Christ. The Herodian spirit worked through generations of Herods, beginning with Herod the Great, who sent soldiers to kill Jesus as a baby, on to Herod Antipas, who had John the Baptist beheaded and sent Jesus to be crucified by Pilate, to Herod Agrippa, who sent the apostle Paul to be martyred in Rome. It was particularly evident throughout this period of history how violently the strong man opposed the Word of truth as God's government began to take hold in the early Church.

As it was then, so it is now. We are crossing over another epic threshold here in the last days before Christ returns. As the government of the Kingdom of God ushered in the manifestation of

His glory after Pentecost (see Acts 2), so will God's divine order bring another wave of glory so that *"all the earth shall be filled with the glory of the Lord"* (Num. 14:21). We are at a turning point in the Church, but God has already declared, *"The glory of this latter temple shall be greater than the former..."* (Hag. 2:9). It has already been foretold that *"the earth will be filled with the knowledge of the glory of the Lord, as the waters cover the sea"* (Hab. 2:14). Though we know the resolution, we must still endure the conflict. Though we know who the victors are, there is still a battle to be waged.

> **We are at a turning point in the Church, but God has already declared, *"The glory of this latter temple shall be greater than the former"* (Hag. 2:9).**

God began to show me the nature of the political spirit and how it was rooted in the events that unfolded around the first coming of Christ. As I saw it embodied in the life of Herod, I began to study Herod and his heritage in more depth. As I already shared with you in Chapter 3, he was an Edomite and descendant of Esau. As I studied the life of Esau, I learned that Esau married Ishmael's daughter. God began to give me some insight into the Muslim world as I studied the life and history of Ishmael. You can read the first part of that message in my book *The Destiny of Islam in the End Times*. Now I will give you a little more insight regarding something that you need to be aware of so that you can exercise your God-given authority to address it. God would not have His end-time Church ignorant as we face the same political

strong man today that opposed Christ and the early Church during the time of the Herods.

Two Roots of Islam

In Islam, from a biblical perspective, there are two roots that
God has to deal with in the earth. One root is the root of Ishmael.
Ishmael was Abraham's son, born of an Egyptian servant, Hagar.
Before instructing Abraham to cast Hagar and Ishmael out at
Sarah's request, God promised, *"Yet I will also make a nation of
the son of the bondwoman, because he is your seed"* (Gen.
21:13). Ishmael, after being cast out of his father's house, married an Egyptian woman and begot 12 princes from whom the
Arab nations are descended. The Muslim people have a heart
that is filled with a void—a void filled with religion rather than
relationship—a void that longs to be filled with the knowledge of
God as a personal *Abba Father* rather than an impersonal *Allah*.
But, like the Jews, until they come to truly know who Christ is,
they are trapped in empty religious practice and are far from
knowing God.

Ishmael, after having been rejected by his father, disinherited, and left in the desert to die, felt abandoned and unworthy. He
was suddenly homeless and without any family. He was crying as
much from a broken heart as from thirst. Yet, while he is lying
under a bush weeping and waiting to die, God hears his cries—
"God heard the voice of the lad…" (Gen. 21:17). The word
Ishmael means, "God will hear."[1] The Lord opens the eyes of his
mother to see a nearby well and she brings him water to drink. As
a result, both of them live (see Gen. 21:19-20). This is a prophetic
parallel to what is happening in the earth today. God is hearing

the cry of the Muslim people who have been in a spiritual wilderness for four thousand years. God is opening their eyes to see the well of salvation that is right before them—namely Jesus. The Church will awaken the longing of the Muslim heart for the love and acceptance of a heavenly Father, but if we ever hope to spoil the house of Islam, we must first bind the strong man who controls it.

The Church will awaken the longing of the Muslim heart for the love and acceptance of a heavenly Father, but if we ever hope to spoil the house of Islam, we must first bind the strong man who controls it.

Yet there is another face that has arisen from an ancient spiritual root in the Muslim world. This expresses itself as terrorism. Nations are wondering what to do about it. The problem is not an external issue for those living in the western world, as we have seen. The threat is not from an enemy who will come from the outside marching in foreign uniforms, but it will arise from within. People living a normal life alongside of you will suddenly answer the call to *jihad* and start building bombs to kill innocent people. But even while living in the midst of this threat, we must be careful about how we deal with it. If all we do is talk about it, preach against it from pulpits, and broadcast how horrible it is in news stories on television and in print media, we are really doing nothing more than promoting the agenda of terrorism. There is but one objective of a terrorist, and that is to instill terror—to plant fear in the heart of God's people.

So what is the answer? We should be asking *who* is the answer, not *what*—and the answer is the same now as it was two thousand years ago when Herod instilled terror throughout the land. It is Jesus Christ, the King of glory, made manifest in the earth. We have an advantage, however: now Jesus resides within every believer. It is the Christ in you that will make manifest God's glory on the earth. Every born-again believer is a vessel of God's honor and glory. It is the people of God, perfected in love, who will hold up a standard against the flood of fear sweeping the world, for *"perfect love casts out fear"* (1 John 4:18). God is allowing the crisis to brew so that the world will come to the Body of Christ and witness that only the love of God and the faith it produces can overcome terror. He wants the Church to have an answer that represents the wisdom and the mindset of Jesus Christ and gives understanding and revelation of the truth.

I believe the day is coming when the governments of this world will come to the Church in their respective nations and ask for help. God will cause the tables to suddenly turn in the darkest hour—the dawn will suddenly break forth. As the prophet said, *"...Your light shall dawn in the darkness, and your darkness shall be as the noonday"* (Isa. 58:10). Whatever it takes, in God's perfect timing, the horizon will align at just the right moment and His light will illuminate the day. As the moon moves across the sky, God is preparing His people. While it is still night, He is teaching and training them and raising them up to be people of stature, ready to give a word of wisdom to the weary.

With my soul I have desired You in the night, yes, by my spirit within me I will seek You early; for when Your judgments are in the earth, the inhabitants of the world will learn righteousness (Isaiah 26:9).

I believe the day is coming when the governments of this world will come to the Church in their respective nations and ask for help.

God is giving His people wisdom and supernatural insight into the spirit realm. He would not have you ignorant of the nature and identity of your enemy. This monster called terrorism has two heads and was spawned by the union of the families of Ishmael and Esau—two oldest sons who were disinherited, cheated out of their birthrights by their younger brothers, and unfairly rejected by their fathers. In Genesis 28:9, Esau marries Ishmael's daughter, although he already had other wives. Esau was Jacob's—or Israel's—elder brother. We know that he sells his birthright to Jacob for a bowl of stew (see Gen. 25:29-34) because he doesn't know how to pass the bread test—to live by every word that proceeds out of the mouth of God. Later, Jacob tricks his father, Isaac, out of the blessing meant for Esau (see Gen. 27:1-29). When Esau returns from hunting the game that he had prepared for his dying father to eat, he discovers his father has already given the blessing of Abraham to his younger brother, Jacob.

Esau is distraught and pleads with Isaac, *"Have you not reserved a blessing for me"* (Gen. 27:36). Isaac could only give the following answer: *"Indeed I have made him your master, and all his brethren I have given to him as servants....What shall I do now for you, my son?" And Esau said to his father, "Have you only one blessing, my father? Bless me—me also, O my father!" and Esau lifted up his voice and wept* (Gen. 27:37-38). Then

Isaac answered him and said, *"By your sword you shall live, and you shall serve your brother; and it shall come to pass, when you become restless, that you shall break his yoke from your neck"* (Gen. 27:40).

So that is Isaac's prophecy over Esau; that he will live by the sword. When Esau marries the daughter of Ishmael, what is in his heart? Genesis 27:41 says that Esau comforts himself with thoughts of killing Jacob. *"So Esau hated Jacob because of the blessing with which his father blessed him, and Esau said in his heart, 'The days of mourning for my father are at hand; then I will kill my brother Jacob.'"* It is a pseudo-comfort that he finds. It is a way to deal with the anguish and pain in his heart. Out of envy, he decides that he will seek revenge. He thinks that, if he can kill Jacob, the pain will be dealt with. The spirit of Esau, or the spirit that he lays hold of, is a spirit that longs to kill Jacob. That is the same spirit that is behind terrorism in Islam today—a spirit that wants first to kill the heirs of Jacob and then also all of those who follow his God.

> **That is the same spirit that is behind terrorism in Islam today—a spirit that wants first to kill the heirs of Jacob and then also all of those who follow his God.**

From Genesis 32:3, we know that Esau went to live *"in the land of Seir, in the country of Edom."* Seir, commonly referred to as "Mt. Seir" in the Bible, is either the Hebrew word *se'ar* for "hair" or "hairy," or *sa'ar,* which means, "to bristle with terror." The Hebrew word *se'ara* means, "to sweep away as in a whirlwind," having the connotation of a storm. In any case, there is an element of fear associated with the word *Seir.* The people of Seir were violent and fierce. The Seirites were known as "The Hairy Warriors" or "Riders On The Storm."[2] This gave all the more reason to fear the Edomites, who kicked the original Seirites out.

Esau was the father of the Edomites. The Edomites have a history of always causing trouble for Israel. Psalm 137:7 (NLT) records that, when Babylon came in to take Jerusalem, the descendents of Esau sided with the invaders. *"Remember what the Edomites did on the day the armies of Babylon captured Jerusalem. 'Destroy it!' they yelled. 'Level it to the ground!' "* That is the nature of the seed of Esau, to kill and destroy through political and religious alliances.

Let's go back for a moment to the legacy of Ishmael. The Ishmaelites settled in the Syrian Desert—in fact, in Hebrew, the word for Arab, *arav*, literally means "desert." Historically, there is a famous *Ismaili* sect from Syria, written about as early as the eighth century, widely known as "the Assassins" or "Holy Killers of Islam." *Isma'il* is Arabic for "Ishmael." In regards to the history of the word Islam—or *Isma'il*—the Etymological Dictionary states: "The Ismailians were not numerous, but among them were the powerful Fatimid dynasty in Egypt and the Assassins, both of whom loomed large in European imagination."[3] The word *assassin* is derived from the Arabic word *hassa,* which means "to kill or exterminate." The medieval headquarters of the Syrian Ismailis was situated on a mountain called *Jabal Assikkin,* or "mountain of the knife," as the word *sikkin* means "knife or dagger."

The Assassins have been described as "a fanatical Ismaili Muslim sect at the time of the Crusades, under the leadership of the 'Old Man of the Mountain' with a reputation for murdering opposing leaders."[4] As a result of the terror they instilled, the Ismailis became famous throughout medieval Europe as "the Assassins," thanks in part to the widely published writings of Barbarossa in the 12th century and Marco Polo in the 13th, hence the modern use of the word *assassin*. Interestingly, Ismaili Assassins were not only notorious for murdering their opponents in public places, but also for sacrificing their lives in the process—a heritage that lives on in modern suicide bombers.

Ever since Esau married Ishmael's daughter, in Genesis 28:9, the seed of Esau and Ishmael has been mingled together. Generations after this time, these two groups of people were connecting with one another even before the religion of Islam came into existence. Islam is only 1,400 years old. The story I am sharing with you about Esau and Ishmael is 4,000 years old.

> **Ishmael's descendents embraced Islam for one reason: it spoke to the void in their heart that God is not a father and could never have a son.**

Ishmael's descendents embraced Islam for one reason: it spoke to the void in their heart that God is not a father and could never have a son. That resonated with the descendents of Ishmael because their own father, Ishmael, had been cast out into the wilderness and left without an inheritance by Abraham, who was a friend of God. Abraham had taught Ishmael about faith, but not about fatherhood—Ishmael walked away from the home where he had come of age, where he had been circumcised at age 13, knowing that there was a God and that he was not worthy to be accepted as a son. The descendants of Ishmael know that Abraham heard from God, and just as Isaac spoke to Esau, the blessing and legacy left to them was one of the sword and servitude. Islam teaches adherents that their best hope is to be counted as a worthy servant in the eyes of God, and that sometimes the best way to serve God is by the sword.

The germ residing in the seed of Ishmael is simply this: whoever God is, He cannot be a father. This issue of fatherlessness is at the root of the woundedness that feeds the bitterness fueling terrorism. You cannot experience any more rejection and abandonment than being disinherited and rejected by a father. In the eyes of Ishmael's descendants, there is no Heavenly Father, only a taskmaster God. They cannot experience a Heavenly Father's love because they could never experience the love of an earthly father. This is the void in the Muslim heart that has been buried and suppressed for 4,000 years.

The last time Ishmael saw his father, after being kicked out of his house, was when he buried him. When he buried his father, he buried any chance of ever experiencing his father's love and acceptance. Esau, like Ishmael, accepted that he would forever live by the sword, with the hope that if he served well in that capacity perhaps God would count him worthy.

Both Ishmael and Esau married Egyptian women. Today Egypt is a Muslim nation. But long before the rise of Islam, Egypt suppressed—and killed—the descendants of Jacob for generations. That is the power of covenant. At the time that

Moses was born, Pharaoh decreed that all the male Hebrew infants be killed. That is the same spirit of Esau—a political spirit—that sought to kill all of the male infants in Judea at the time that Jesus was born. When Islam began to expand throughout the Arab world about 1,400 years ago, emanating from Saudi Arabia just across the Red Sea from Egypt, it represented a religious covenant between all the descendants of Esau and Ishmael. While Ishmael had said in his heart, "God is not a father, but I can find an identity as a servant; I can find justification through works," the descendents of Esau said, "I shall live by the sword as a means to vindicate myself." The sons of Esau embraced Islam as a means to express the violence in their hearts and their desire to kill the seed of Jacob.

These are the two roots of Islam. On the one hand, we have the seed of Ishmael crying out in the desert for a father's love and validation; on the other, we have the seed of Esau crying out for blood and retribution. The Church must be careful not to paint the entire Muslim world with the spirit of violence passed down through the seed of Esau—that is only half of the story.

The Second Face of Esau

The seed of Esau has two faces. One is the face of terrorism, which you have been reading about, and the other is the political spirit. The political spirit is the invisible mastermind behind terrorism and Islam. This strong man in disguise can only be discerned supernaturally. This same spirit is also operating here in the West but with a different expression; it is the same strong man—or political spirit—that we learned operated through Herod. This Herodian spirit is at work making alliances with the pharisaical—or religious—spirit in the Church, along with the Jezebel spirit, to thwart and destroy the plan of God. Wherever this strong man has dominion in the western Church, the path will be paved for Islam to enter in and have dominion in that nation. God showed me that this is taking place most particularly in the United States, Canada, Great Britain, and other European Nations.

> **Wherever this strong man has dominion in the western Church, the path will be paved for Islam to enter in and have dominion in that nation.**

While on the surface we are focusing on the overt operations of terrorism, a snake is making inroads underground with the agenda of taking territory in the western Church. The Lord showed me that, wherever this strong man gets a foothold and the Church neglects to deal with it in her own backyard, she will not have the earned authority to deal with Islam and the spirit of Esau when it comes in full force.

We cannot effectively begin to reach out to Ishmael as a nation until we deal with this strong man. Scripture says that you cannot go into a house and spoil the goods of the enemy unless you have first bound the strong man—and you can't bind the strong man unless you are stronger than he is (see Matt. 12:29). You read in Chapters 2 and 3 that the strong man is the one under whom all the other spirits operate. It is not enough to deal with a spirit that is operating underneath, or in alliance with, the strong man because the strong man will sacrifice that other spirit to save itself; and then it will come back with reinforcements later on. You must bind the strong man in order to put an end to its schemes once and for all. But the strong man not only has to be bound, it also has to be replaced with a stronger power, which is the government of Jesus Christ. In order to change a nation, you have to change the government. The political spirit that has crept into the western Church is the spirit that God wants to displace so that He can establish His ways in preparation for His final outreach upon the earth.

The Lord spoke to me and said that wherever the political spirit has dominion the nation of Islam will prevail. If the Church in the western world does not conquer the political spirit in her own backyard, then how will she have the authority to deal with the Nation of Islam already at her door?

Remember that the political spirit we face is actually the same spirit that is behind the terrorism that we are familiar with today. It is the same spirit, but with a different face—and a more lethal, slicker mode of operation. One makes way for the other. If we are to end terrorism, we must bind the strongman behind Islam. Then once he is bound, we must usher in the government of God—the worldwide evangelization of the Muslim world with the Gospel of Jesus Christ.

If we are to see the end-time harvest, we must bind the strongman behind Islam.

God told me, "I want to prepare My people, and I want to position and posture them to deal with this strong man, because the nation that comes to oppose them is ripe for harvest…. I only need a remnant among My people who will come into alignment in order to address this evil." God will raise up that remnant. This is the assignment. God wants to bring victory.

I know that some of you reading this book are called to reach millions or to be distribution centers of wealth to reach millions, but you are not doing it yet because you can't get through an invisible ceiling. You may already know that you are dealing with a political spirit, but you need to know how to overcome it before you can transition into the next phase of your destiny. God wants to put some tools in your hand so that you can triumph over this strong man and begin to move forward. We will discuss these tools in detail later in the book.

The Five Strategies of Terrorism

We know that God is not a respecter of people and that whoever calls upon the name of the Lord shall be saved. ...*God shows no partiality. But in every nation whoever fears Him and works righteousness is accepted by Him. ...That, through His name, whoever believes in Him will receive remission of sins* (Acts 10:34-35,43). I am not talking about a natural lineage to make you think that anyone with the seed of Esau in their heritage is a terrorist. I am showing you the roots of a spiritual lineage at work in the spiritual realm. The root motive of this spirit behind terrorism is that it seeks to kill Jacob. But that is only one face of the spirit of terrorism that we see in the world today.

Another face—or strategy—of terrorism is that it seeks to make the Church deaf to the cry of the Muslim heart—or to the cry of Ishmael. It wants the Church to become deaf and dull of hearing so that we do not hear Ishmael crying out in the wilderness and then go to meet that cry with the Gospel. The only way to hear the voice of Ishmael in this era is by revelation of the Spirit. This is because the western world has become hard of hearing concerning the Muslim people. It is something that we must repent of and allow the Spirit of God to heal in us.

The spirit of terrorism wants to camouflage the destiny of the Muslim nations so that we don't see them in the light of Scripture.

The spirit of terrorism wants to camouflage the destiny of the Muslim nations so that we don't see them in the light of Scripture. God wants to touch them in the end-times like he touched Saul of Tarsus. Saul had a head-on collision with glory and became the apostle Paul—God used him to provoke God's people—the Jews—to a passion. Paul had to suffer many things because he poked and prodded and stirred the Church to life. But before he became an apostle, he was a terrorist. He didn't have guns or bombs, but he had stones and a religious agenda. He wreaked havoc on the first followers of Christ. He was there at Stephen's death and afterward continued to hunt down, imprison, and beat all who believed in the Lord. This man was a problem, and most people in the Church probably would have said, "Lord, get rid of Saul." But instead God had a chosen purpose for Saul. Who would have believed that the Church's greatest persecutor would become her greatest advocate?

We need to have an understanding of God's corporate heart. Corporately He is doing bigger things than any one of us can fathom. He loves us individually as if we are each His only child, but God is dealing with times and seasons on a corporate level in the earth as well. There are campaigns and strategies taking place in the spirit that we cannot discern with our natural eyes. There are eternal purposes that He is fulfilling in our midst. There is an end-time purpose to the terrorism that we are witnessing—it is the cry of Muslims, to God, to be right with Him.

So the spirit of terrorism not only seeks to destroy the seed of Jacob, but also to paralyze the Church with fear. A primary strategy of terrorism is to paralyze. It uses fear as a tool to immobilize the Church—because while love mobilizes, fear paralyzes. It uses the same paralyzing, deafening fear to cause misunderstanding and upheaval within the Muslim world. There is no clear "on behalf of whom" sense of loyalty with this spirit. Terrorism is as intent on destroying Jacob and the Church as it is on destroying the lives of those it recruits to do it. It preys upon the multitudes of disillusioned Muslim youths living in confusion and uncertainty.

This is yet another strategy of the spirit of terrorism. It convinces a lost generation that they can become heroes by wrapping a bomb around their chest and promises that they will wake up in the next life surrounded by 72 virgins. Joining the Jihadist ranks offers a false sense of purpose, identity, and comfort. The enemy behind terrorism is after a generation of fatherless men in search of meaning and hope. The Church has not given them either, and now the Lord is saying, "I want My people to speak to them before the enemy does, because the enemy will offer a self-destructive, counterfeit servitude rather than authentic, life-affirming sonship."

And yet there is still another strategy of terrorism. The spirit behind terrorism is intent on depleting the financial blessings of Ishmael that are stored up for the end-time harvest. God told Abraham that He would bless Ishmael and make him a great nation.

> *And as for Ishmael, I have heard you. Behold, I have blessed him, and will make him fruitful, and will multiply him exceedingly. He shall beget twelve princes, and I will make him a great nation* (Genesis 17:20).

Great wealth has been stored up in the Middle East. The oil that has been placed in the hands of the Muslim people is because of the unconditional blessing that God spoke over Ishmael's descendants—it is for an end-time purpose. The enemy is working double time to deplete these stores of wealth by diverting them to fund terrorism. One out of every three barrels of oil from Saudi Arabia, for example, ends up in the pockets of terrorist organizations.[5]

There is no other source of wealth in the Middle East other than oil. No invention or new technology has come out of an Arab nation in the last 500 years. They are completely reliant on oil to finance whatever they aspire to do. Of course, there is a huge disparity between those few who control the oil and the rest of the population, which is why we have an army of lost and impoverished youth with no other reason to live than to kill. Because of this, the terrorists are getting recruits with their promises that these youths can live in paradise if they die killing for the cause of Islam. It would seem that Ishmael's blessing has turned into the world's curse—but what the enemy has meant for harm, the Lord will use for good. God wants to set apart those finances because He is going to use them for the end-time harvest. *If the Church will fund the harvest of the Muslim world, the Muslim world will fund the harvest of the Jewish people.*

Another strategy of terrorism is to keep Abraham's first son from returning home and fulfilling his eternal purpose. The destiny of Ishmael is to cause Israel's eyes to be opened and the scales to fall off, because nothing else will provoke Israel to jealousy for the Messiah like Ishmael coming into the Kingdom of God first. God has an end-time destiny for Ishmael that no force can stop. Not only does God want to see the Muslim people saved, but He also wants the whole earth to be saved so that none should perish. It is the will of God that *all* would come to repentance. That is the corporate heart of God.

> **Not only does God want to see the Muslim people saved, but He also wants the whole earth to be saved so that none should perish. It is the will of God that all would come to repentance. That is the corporate heart of God.** 2 Pet 3:9

There is also the strategic heart of God. How is God going to usher in the final harvest when entire regions of the earth—whole hemispheres of the planet—are opposed to the Gospel? He will accomplish it by causing the eyes of the Muslim people to be opened. When the Muslim world at last drinks from the wells of salvation—when 42 percent of the world's unsaved population receives a revelation of Christ—and that body of wealth comes into God's Kingdom to advance the Gospel, every other realm will be affected. The strong man will be forced to relinquish his strongholds in every part of the world. God will send the Muslim people back into a complacent western Church to provoke her to a passion for Jesus, and together they will bring the seed of Jacob back home to the Father.

Through the Church, God wants to raise up an army to reach out to Ishmael—because it is Ishmael who will reach out to Israel. The last people on earth that Israel expects God to reach out His hand to is their archenemy, Ishmael, who has surrounded and hunted and harassed them throughout history. While Israel and the Church call upon God to reprove the Muslim world, God has another plan. Yes, the cup of wrath has been filling up before the throne—the day of wrath will come—but the cup of mercy has been overflowing for two thousand years. The door to salvation is open to anyone who comes to Him. That is how you came to the knowledge of Christ—it was His goodness that led you to repentance. *"Or do you despise the riches of His goodness, forbearance, and longsuffering, not knowing that the goodness of God leads you to repentance?"* (Rom. 2:4).

Through His mercy, God will also lead Israel; but first He will provoke them to jealousy. He will use the Gentiles, foremost of whom are the Arab nations. In Romans 11:11, Paul said, *"...To provoke them to jealousy, salvation has come to the Gentiles."* In order for Israel to be jealous for God, the Gentiles must be saved. Gentiles are strangers to the covenant of Israel. There is no greater Gentile than the Muslim people—or Ishmael—in the eyes of Israel because, for their sake, for Isaac's sake, Ishmael was cast out. But Ishmael will be brought into God's Kingdom for Israel's sake. That is why the destiny of the Muslim world and their connection to what God is about to do is so significant. That is why the spirit of terrorism has raised its head. Terrorism wants to camouflage the destiny of Islam connected to the endtimes, but God is exposing every hidden motive. *"...For there is nothing covered that will not be revealed, and hidden that will not be known"* (Matt. 10:26).

God is allowing terrorism to be exposed so that it will cause the Church and Israel and all the nations of the world to look into the spirit and ask, "What is going on?" God is getting the attention of the world—and when He has their undivided attention, He will make His final move.

Meditation Points

- How does the spirit behind Islam relate to the political spirit operating in the West? What are some characteristics of Islam that have been handed down from Ishmael and Esau? Considering these things, what should you be praying for the Muslim world today?

- Remember that where the political spirit has dominion Islam will prevail.

- What do the five strategies of terrorism reveal to you about the work of the political spirit?

- What terrorism means for evil, God will turn to good. Pray over this end-time harvest of the Muslim world and ask God to open doors, reveal His strategies, and equip His people to accomplish them.

Endnotes

1. Faisal Malick, *Destiny of Islam in the End Times,* (Shippensburg, PA: Destiny Image Publishers, 2008).

2. "Meaning, origin and etymology of the name Seir," *Abarim Publications*, http://www.abarim-publications.com/Meaning/Seir.html (accessed 29 August 2008).

3. *Online Etymological Dictionary*, s.v. "Islam," http://www.etymonline.com/index.php?search=ishmael (accessed 30 August 2008).

4. *Ibid.*, s.v. "Assassin," http://www.etymonline.com/index.php?search=assassin (accessed 30 August 2008).

5. Malick, *Destiny of Islam in the End Times.*

Chapter 6

THE FINAL BATTLE FOR POWER

They will come from the east and the west,
from the north and the south, and sit down
in the kingdom of God. And indeed there
are last who will be first, and there are
first who will be last (Luke 13:29-30).

First Corinthians 10:32 tells us, *"Don't give offense to Jews or Gentiles or the church of God"* (NLT). These are the three groups of people in the earth. Before Jesus came, there were only two groups: the Jews and the Gentiles. Before there were the Jews, there were only Gentiles.

If we begin with Noah after the Flood, where humankind starts all over again, we see the origin of 70 different nations (see Gen. 10:1-32). Eight generations later, when God came to Abraham and preached the Gospel to him, He said, *"...In you and in your seed all the families of the earth shall be blessed"*

(Gen. 28:14). God's heart has always been for the nations. He established a covenant to bless the nations through the seed of Abraham, which we know has manifested through the person of Jesus Christ. Salvation has come to every nation once and for all through the blood of the Lamb.

In Luke 13, immediately before Jesus is told by the Pharisees that Herod Antipas wants to kill Him, Jesus has just finished explaining that, *People will come from east and west and north and south, and will take their places at the feast in the kingdom of God. Indeed there are those who are last who will be first, and first who will be last* (Luke 13:29-30 NIV). This principle greatly upsets the Pharisees and they tell Him, *"Leave this place and go somewhere else. Herod wants to kill you"* (Luke 13:31 NIV).

We see this truth in operation from the time that God makes his covenant with Abraham. God separated Abraham from the nations and made Abraham first and the nations last. Then He separated Isaac from Ishmael and made Isaac first and Ishmael last. Then he separated Jacob by divine election from his older brother Esau. And even Jacob's son Joseph, who was last among his brothers, sold into slavery, and then thrown into prison, became first in command in Egypt and the savior of his family and the Middle East. Now we have the Jewish people, God's chosen, who will be the last to enter the Kingdom of God—while the Gentiles, including the Muslims, *"...who seem least important now will be the greatest then..."* (Luke 13:30 NLT). As I have said, the sons of Ishmael will usher in the end-time harvest and cause the scales to fall from the eyes of Israel. This is why we are told not to give offense to the Gentiles in First Corinthians 10:32.

God also said to be careful about our attitude toward the Jewish people because *"...blindness in part has happened to Israel until the fullness of the Gentiles has come"* (Rom. 11:25). The blindness of Israel is for a reason and a season only. When Israel is provoked to jealousy by the fullness of the Gentiles, they will seek that fullness for themselves. God wants to bring about the end-time harvest so that He can reveal Himself to Israel. But you can't have a harvest of the Gentile nations without the Muslim world because 42 percent of the Gentile population on the earth is Muslim. You aren't going to have "fullness of the Gentiles" without the Muslim people. Once we see the fullness of the Gentiles come into God's Kingdom, we will begin to see the salvation of Israel.

> **You can't have a harvest of the Gentile nations without the Muslim world because 42 percent of the Gentile population on the earth is Muslim. You aren't going to have "fullness of the Gentiles" without the Muslim people.**

Isaiah 60 tells us that *"The Gentiles shall come to your light, and kings to the brightness of your rising. ...The wealth of the Gentiles shall come to you"* (Isa. 60:3,5). Isaiah then names the sons of Ishmael: Kedar, Nebaioth, and others (see Isa. 60:7). All that we read in Isaiah 60 is a prophecy regarding the Muslim world. They are going to come to the rising of the Church, but first the Church has to arise in glory for them to see her. The

Church will not be filled with the glory of God until the strong man is bound and expelled from her midst.

Binding the Strong Man of Terrorism

Obadiah 1:21 says, *"Then saviors shall come to Mount Zion to judge the mountains of Esau, and the kingdom shall be the Lord's."* What is a mountain? A mountain speaks of government and dominion. When you conquer a mountain, you conquer the high places. Whatever happens at the mountaintop will happen at the foot of the mountain. The mountains of Esau represent the primary objectives of terrorism: to take out Israel—or Jacob— and to take out the Church.

The Church has to be postured and positioned in authority to deal with this spirit so that the strong man that is keeping the Muslim people hostage can be bound and so that the descendants of Ishmael can be adopted into the family of God. Once they come in, God's eternal purpose for Israel will begin to take place.

In Matthew 16:18 the Lord says, *"...I will build my church, and the gates of hell shall not prevail against it"* (ESV). If gates are open that are releasing hell, the Church has to open gates that will release Heaven. The enemy is organized. It is not divided against itself. Jesus said that if a kingdom is divided against itself it will fall (see Mark 3:24). Therefore, the Church has to be united in what we understand the mind of Christ to be; we must also share the heart of the Father. When the heart and the mind come together, we will begin to have precision and accuracy in our operation, and then we can take territory for Jesus Christ.

The heart of God is to show mercy, and the mind of Christ is to reveal truth. Glory will dwell in the land when mercy and truth come together (see Ps. 85:9-10). We are told in Psalm 57:3 that *"God shall send forth His mercy and His truth"* and then, two verses later, that His glory will be over all the earth (see Ps. 57:5). We learn from John 1:14 that *"the Word became flesh and dwelt among us...full of grace and truth"* and, a few verses later, that while *"the law was given through Moses, but grace and truth came through Jesus Christ"* (John 1:17). Where mercy and truth are in operation, the strong man is bound and silenced. Where righteousness and peace are, the government of the Kingdom of God is in operation.

On the contrary, the heart and mind of the strong man behind terrorism are death and deception—its thought is to deceive and its intent is to kill. As the letter of the law—legalism—kills without the mercy of the Spirit, so does the political spirit. We know the political spirit is at work establishing false government wherever criticism, condemnation, and mistrust are prevalent. This is what King Herod yielded to when Jesus came on the scene, just as King Saul did when David showed up. Murder arose in their hearts because the seed of Jacob was on the move. When the seed of Jacob arises, it causes the seed of Esau to arise. *"We do not wrestle against flesh and blood, but against principalities..."* (Eph. 6:12). The powers against which we war are bent on killing the seed of Jacob.

We know the political spirit is at work establishing false government wherever criticism, condemnation, and mistrust are prevalent.

The POLITICAL *Spirit*

The Islamic strong man is rearing his head in the world today because the seed of Jacob is about to rise up for good. The political spirit will always attempt to establish false government before true government comes, especially in the Church. Anytime a false government is being established, God drops a plumb line so that He can separate the false from the true that He wants to establish. God is doing this in the earth right now.

We must be discerning. The Lord is warning His people that the political spirit is gaining territory in the western Church. If we do not deal with the strong man of the political spirit in the western Church, when the nation of Islam comes, we will not have the authority to be able to handle it. This is because we will have given dominion over to the political spirit by allowing false government to take control. If we allow the strong man to establish power as Herod did, we won't be left with any governmental authority to displace it. This is the spirit that the Church must deal with as a united Body. There is too much at stake to be complacent. We are talking about Israel's destiny, Ishmael's destiny, and God's end-time purpose for the Church.

God wants to establish an apostolic government with dominion in order to deal with this spirit. There is only one way that can be achieved—and that is with the wisdom of God. This is why Ephesians 3:10 says that *"now the manifold wisdom of God might be made known by the church to the principalities and powers in the heavenly places."* When principalities and powers hear hidden wisdom, which was foreordained before the foundation of the world, uttered by lips of clay, it catches them off guard and renders them powerless. The wisdom of God is to be made known *through the Church,* even to principalities and powers.

Once the wisdom of God is made known, there is no other wisdom that can stand against it.

The Bible says in First Corinthians 3:19, *"The wisdom of this world is foolishness with God. For it is written, 'He catches the wise in their own craftiness.' "* You see, while Herod wanted to kill Jesus, God used the spirit of Herod to position Jesus in Egypt so that *"it might be fulfilled which was spoken by the Lord through the prophet, saying, 'Out of Egypt I called My Son' "* (Matt. 2:15). That is the wise being taken in their own craftiness.

The cross of Christ is the wisdom of God.

You will never step into destiny until you tap into the wisdom of God in order to conquer this spirit. While Herod was trying to push his agenda, God made it clear that He would take the wise in their own craftiness. In First Corinthians 2:7-8, the Bible says that the rulers of darkness did not know the Lord of Glory—nor did they know the wisdom of God—or they would *not* have crucified Christ. The cross of Christ is the wisdom of God.

The Time Is at Hand

The political spirit behind Islam does not know any barriers. Religious and political alliances are all the same to it. It will come with a religious face and seem to promote the Church's agenda, but this is just a means to an end. It will use churches not wise to its tactics for its own purposes. The "seeker friendly" churches that have become so popular are an example of this. They are a mile wide and an inch deep, meaning that they attract large congregations, but don't teach any deep truths. They are "feel good" churches that steer clear of difficult messages regarding faith and righteousness. They do not challenge the complacency of our wealthy nations to reach out sacrificially to a world that needs the Gospel. Political correctness takes precedence over uprightness before God. They are more political in nature than truly Christian, and as such, they will fall as easy prey to the political spirit since they operate in the very same manner to build their churches.

The universal Church is weakened when it attempts to use these political means to promote itself. When denominational Christianity makes alliances with politicians, it will be used to forward political agendas rather than the Gospel of Jesus Christ. Church leaders are deceived into thinking that, by joining political ranks, by locking arms with political leaders, they will advance the Kingdom of God. When religion and politics join forces, there will be corruption in both arenas. This is the very nature and goal of the political spirit.

This is how the political spirit operating in the western Church relates to the strong man behind Islam. You may be wondering, if the same spirit working through Islam is infiltrating the Church on a political level, then how can one believer—or one body of believers—stem the tide? Let me assure you that the political spirit in the Church is much weaker than the political spirit operating throughout the Islamic world simply because there is no separation of church and state in Muslim countries. In the West, the religious and political spirits have to make a network of alliances on all sorts of levels in order for the political spirit to gain a foothold. This is not true in nations under Sharia Law.

It is easy to think that those alliances will never happen in the western world, but they are happening. Politically, the Herodian spirit is making inroads into the Church and creating alliances with the religious spirit and the Jezebel spirit. Because we are not confronting the work of the strong man in these areas, it is acquiring domain.

However, God is saying that, if you and I will bind the strong man in our midst, on the lowest level, wherever we see these alliances taking place, then God will give us—God's people— authority in the nation of Islam. It is a matter of taking dominion in the small areas—beginning in our own homes and church communities—in order to have authority in the larger arenas of the world's political systems.

In my spirit, I see the nation of Islam coming, but I also see that they will encounter resistance in the spirit realm. If we rise up and conquer this political spirit in the Church, the spirit behind Islam will hit the hand of God and be denied access into the West. When this happens, we will see the end-time harvest begin in earnest.

If we rise up and conquer this political spirit in the Church, the spirit behind Islam will hit the hand of God and be denied access into the West. When this happens, we will see the end-time harvest begin in earnest.

The time is at hand. In previous eras, when revelation came about the Jezebel spirit in the Church, people got a hold of it and began to pray. Prayer is always the first step. The Church prayed, and God exposed the Jezebel spirit everywhere. I am not talking about exposing individual people; I am talking about dealing with a corporate enemy that God wants us to overcome. This entails more than rebuking; it involves an overcoming by taking authority and establishing divine government that reflects the corporate heart of God. We have already been given authority; we simply need to tap into God's strategy for implementing it.

With knowledge comes responsibility. If you are mindful to heed what you hear, God will continue to give you more insight and guidance. Don't think that you can accomplish your assignment if you don't help deal with this spirit working against the Church. But be careful not to look at people—remember we do not war against flesh and blood. Do not put yourself in the position of judging whether someone is yielding to a political spirit or not. We are not dealing with people; we are dealing with an entity. This spirit uses people who are naïve or ignorant but well meaning—they may innocently yield to it, believing they are submitting to authority and by doing so honoring God. They may empower a Jezebel spirit simply because they are blind to it. Your job is not to condemn. You may identify someone who is yielding to a political spirit, but that will not change it. Condemning another person will never give you the victory that you need to fulfill the mandate that God has given you.

We are all sons and daughters of a loving Heavenly Father. We are called to be imitators of Him who loved us first, while we were yet sinners (see Rom. 5:8). We are called to walk in love with one another (see John 13:34). Rely on the love of God that is already at work within you, and pray for wisdom. Pray that God would take the wise in their own craftiness. Pray according to Luke 8:17 that *"nothing is secret that will not be revealed, nor anything hidden that will not be known and come to light."* Pray that God would expose the political spirit in our day. Pray that the Church will be empowered to bind the strong man, displace it, and replace it with godly government and leadership (see Matt. 12:29).

You and I have stepped into a corporate Kingdom assignment. Pray daily for discernment, wisdom, and mercy. *"Be sober, be vigilant; because your adversary the devil walks about like a roaring lion, seeking whom he may devour"* (1 Pet. 5:8). The Kingdom of God is at hand; for this reason, we must *"not be unwise, but understand what the will of the Lord is"* (Eph. 5:17). We have to understand the mind of Christ, for it is only the wisdom of God that will triumph over the political spirit and its principalities.

Meditation Points

- How can you take leadership in your sphere of influence or organization to recognize the work of the political spirit and bind the strong man? How can this undergird the plan of God to reach the Muslim world with the Gospel?

- How can you work to develop true unity in the Body of Christ in your area? What do you need to do to make sure you are walking in love, not judging other people, and aligning with God's will to fight this battle in the spiritual realm?

- Pray daily for wisdom and discernment to see things through Jesus' eyes and to have mercy toward those that oppose you until they themselves meet Jesus as Paul did on the road to Damascus.

Chapter 7

GOD'S SECRET WEAPON

*...I should preach among the Gentiles the
unsearchable riches of Christ...to the intent
that now the manifold wisdom of God might be
made known by the church to the principalities
and powers in the heavenly places, according to
the eternal purpose which He accomplished in
Christ Jesus our Lord* (Ephesians 3:8,10-11).

The eternal purpose of the enemy is to oppose the establishment of God's Kingdom on the earth. The enemy that sets itself against the government of God is the strong man that I have identified as the political spirit. It is the spirit that worked through Herod to try to keep the Son of Man from being born—upon whose shoulders divine government would be established—and then to kill Him once it saw that He was alive and growing stronger. It is the spirit that is working through Islam today to keep the Body of Christ from walking in the fullness of God's glory and bringing *"salvation to the ends of the earth"* (Acts 13:47).

The political spirit did not succeed in preventing the Word from entering the earth in the person of Jesus, nor did it succeed in silencing it after Jesus was crucified—the Church continued preaching the Good News on Christ's behalf endued with the power of His resurrection. Nor will the political spirit succeed in keeping the knowledge of the glory of God from filling the earth in the last days. God's government will be established, and Christ will reign with His Bride, the Church, at His side.

We already know the end of the story. God's Word will prevail, and His government will be established. Through the prophet Isaiah, God promised, *"My word...that goes forth from My mouth...shall not return to Me void, but it shall accomplish what I please, and it shall prosper in the thing for which I sent it"* (Isa. 55:11). Isaiah also declared, *"Of the increase of His government and peace there will be no end..."* (Isa. 9:7). That said, what should we, as His Church, be doing in the meantime?

Ephesians 3:10-11 states that the Church is to make God's wisdom known to powers and principalities: *To the intent **that now the manifold wisdom of God might be made known by the church to the principalities and powers in the heavenly places**, according to the eternal purpose which He accomplished in Christ Jesus our Lord.* It is God's eternal purpose for the Church, which He set the groundwork for through Christ. It is a lofty mandate, but as Jesus said so many times, *"...with God all things are possible"* (see Matt. 19:26; Mark 10:27, Luke 18:27). Jesus added this caveat in Mark 9:23: *"...all things are possible to him who believes"* (emphasis added). So again, we each have a role in bringing the purposes of God to pass.

After Jesus went to be with the Father and sent the Holy Spirit to be with the Church, His disciples ministered with a new boldness and authority. Peter, James, John, and eventually Paul, operated with an apostolic anointing that brought the glory of God to bear in a variety of situations. They spread the Good News of the Gospel, announced that the Kingdom of God was at hand, and organized the new Body of believers into what would become the early Church. In doing so, the political spirit was provoked. It continued to work through the Herodian Dynasty as the early Church grew and increased in wisdom, knowledge, and stature. It tried to silence the apostles and quench the move of the Spirit, but at first, it did not succeed.

How did the first apostles gain victory over the political spirit working through Herod—and how will the Church gain victory over the same spirit still opposing Christ today? Remember, as we are fighting wickedness in heavenly places, we must also keep in mind that *"the god of this age has blinded the minds of unbelievers, so that they cannot see the light of the gospel of the glory of Christ..."* (2 Cor. 4:4 NIV). The Church must fight an enemy that cannot be seen while at the same time the world is blinded to the one thing that can overcome it: namely, the wisdom of God.

Let's take a deeper look at how God has positioned the Church to reveal God's wisdom, and in doing so, to dismantle the enemy's strongholds once and for all.

Embracing Wisdom

In Proverbs 21:22 you will read, *"A wise man scales the city of the mighty, and brings down the trusted stronghold."* To bring down the enemy's stronghold, you have to use wisdom. Listen to this illustration:

> *There was a little city with few men in it; and a great king came against it, besieged it, and built great snares around it. Now there was found in it a poor wise man, and he by his wisdom delivered the city...* (Ecclesiastes 9:14-15).

Solomon goes on to explain that *"wisdom is better than strength...wisdom is better than weapons of war"* (Eccles. 9:16,18). In between these two statements, however, he warns that too often wisdom is despised or goes unheard. *"Words of the wise, spoken quietly, should be heard rather than the shout of a ruler of fools"* (Eccl. 9:17). This reminds me of Paul's instructions to the Ephesians when he writes, *"We should no longer be children, tossed to and fro and carried about with every wind of doctrine, by the trickery of men, in the cunning craftiness of deceitful plotting"* (Eph. 4:14). This is the difference between the wisdom of the world and the wisdom of Heaven. Worldly wisdom and cunning will never bring victory against the political spirit— you will never beat the enemy at his own game.

The only force that can outmaneuver the political spirit is the wisdom of God.

The only force that can outmaneuver the political spirit is the wisdom of God. Proverbs 21:30 plainly states, *"There is no wisdom, no insight, no plan that can succeed against the Lord"* (NIV). There are no schemes, plans, plots, or demonic strategies that can succeed against God's wisdom—no human, earthly, or demonic wisdom or counsel will bring success. The only way to defeat the political spirit is to access and harness divine wisdom.

You need to understand the different types of wisdom in order to discern what genuine, godly wisdom is. There are three kinds of wisdom at work in the world. First, there is earthly wisdom—or human wisdom. In First Corinthians 1:17, Paul states that man's wisdom makes the cross of Christ of no effect: *"Preach the gospel—not with words of human wisdom, lest the cross of Christ be emptied of its power"* (NIV). The wisdom of man makes sense to your physical senses and human reasoning—it feels good, looks good, and seems rational, but it is not the wisdom of God, and it will lead you down the wrong path. As Proverbs 14:12 says, *"There is a way that seems right to a man, but its end is the way of death."* It is dictated by the desires of your flesh, your intellect, or the people around you. If you are to walk in God's fullness, you must *"...cease from your own [human] wisdom"* (Prov. 23:4 AMP). *"Beware lest anyone cheat you through philosophy and empty deceit, according to the tradition of men, according to the basic principles of the world, and not according to Christ"* (Col. 2:8).

The second type of wisdom is demonic or satanic wisdom. James explains, *"This is not the kind of wisdom that comes from God. But this wisdom comes from the world...and from the devil"* (James 3:15 NLV). He says that this wisdom is sensual and devilish in nature. You will operate according to this type of wisdom *"if you have bitter envy and self-seeking in your hearts"* (James 3:14). This is a dangerous sort of wisdom, *"For where envy and self-seeking exist, confusion and every evil thing are there"* (James 3:16).

The third kind of wisdom is the wisdom of God. *"We speak wisdom among those who are mature, yet not the wisdom of this age, nor of the rulers of this age, who are coming to nothing. But we speak the wisdom of God..."* (1 Cor. 2:6-7). It is the wisdom of God that brings victory. You will recognize God's wisdom because *"The wisdom that is from above is first pure, then peaceable, gentle, willing to yield, full of mercy and good fruits, without partiality and without hypocrisy"* (James 3:17). It is available to every believer. James writes, *"If any of you lacks wisdom, let him ask of God, who gives to all liberally and without reproach..."* (James 1:5). When the wisdom of Heaven is in operation, any other type of wisdom is immediately exposed as foolishness. The key to victory is to gain access to and operate from the wisdom of God. This is your first line of defense against the false, devilish wisdom of the political spirit.

It is the wisdom of God that brings victory.

We opened this chapter with Ephesians 3:10: *"That now the manifold wisdom of God might be made known by the church to the principalities and powers in the heavenly places."* God's original intent is that, through the Church, His manifold wisdom would be made known to principalities and powers. What is manifold wisdom exactly?

When you were in school, did you ever see one of those origami-type contraptions that had different panels that would appear as you opened and closed it? It was made of pieces of paper folded inward and backward; you could twist and turn it as you closed and opened it to expose a different set of panels every time. Just like that "many-folded" gadget, there are many "folds" of God's wisdom. That is the *manifold* wisdom of God. With every twist and turn, a new facet of God's wisdom is revealed. It is never ending.

The further back you look into eternity past, you will see the wisdom of God in operation. Before the foundations of the world, God established and set into motion the many folds of wisdom that the Church would need to bring victory in the last days. His intention is for the Church to make that wisdom known.

If you are stepping into a divine purpose and moving into that sphere of influence, then the sovereign hand of the Lord will come upon you for a divine assignment. A grace will come upon you through which God will sovereignly start to work in your life. Have you ever noticed, looking back over your life, even to the time before you were saved, that you are able to see the fingerprints of God all along the way? You can see how God preserved you when you weren't even paying attention. He was working out an assignment. God is always working through His manifold wisdom.

Look again at what happened in the life of Jesus. While He was yet a baby, Herod sought to kill him. So God warns Joseph in a dream and Jesus ends up in Egypt *"until the death of Herod that it might be fulfilled which was spoken by the Lord through the prophet, saying, 'Out of Egypt I called my son' "* (Matt. 2:15).

While they are still in Egypt, an angel of the Lord appears to Joseph again and tells him that it is time to go back to Israel because the Herod that sought the boy's life is now dead. As soon as they return to Israel, Joseph learns that Herod's son, Archelaus, is now ruling over Judea. Joseph is again divinely warned in a dream and takes his family to Galilee. He ends up in Nazareth, thereby fulfilling another Messianic prophecy: *"He came and dwelt in a city called Nazareth, that it might be fulfilled which was spoken by the prophets, 'He shall be called a Nazarene' "* (Matt. 2:23).

As a young boy, Jesus begins walking in the wisdom of God. We know from Luke 2:52 that *"Jesus increased in wisdom and stature, and in favor with God and men."* At the same time, Herod Antipas is rising to power and getting into position to oppose Him. Yet all the while, God is using Herod to fulfill His purpose for Jesus. That is the wisdom of God. God is taking the wise in their own craftiness.

Paul explains in First Corinthians 2:7-8 that the wisdom of God is a mystery in order to confound the enemy: *...The hidden wisdom which God ordained before the ages for our glory, which none of the rulers of this age knew; for had they known, they would not have crucified the Lord of glory.* If the rulers of darkness had been aware of God's plan, they would never have crucified Christ. The strong man played right into God's hand. He enabled Jesus to fulfill His destiny on earth by allowing Him to be crucified so that you and I might be receive eternal life and fulfill all of the will of God.

If the rulers of darkness had been aware of God's plan, they would never have crucified Christ. The strong man played right into God's hand.

You might wonder, if Jesus dealt with this spirit and ended up crucified, will that be your end too? Fortunately, that sacrifice has already been taken care of by Christ. Whatever God calls you to do, however, you will have the grace required to accomplish it. God said, *"My grace is sufficient for you, for My strength is made perfect in weakness..."* (2 Cor. 12:9). With God's wisdom comes His grace. Know that, if God is the one calling and anointing you, then *"your life is hidden with Christ"* (Col. 3:3) and any enemy opposing you will come against the sovereign hand of God before it can ever touch you.

Be sure of who you are in Christ; then you can rest in Him, knowing that He will give you wisdom, that His hand will back you, and that He will remove any barriers out of your way so that you can fulfill your assignment.

Embrace wisdom by trusting the Word of God and resting in the knowledge of Christ. Don't be wise in your own eyes, but fear the Lord (see Prov. 3:7) for *"the fear of the Lord is the beginning of wisdom, and the knowledge of the Holy One is understanding"* (Prov. 9:10). Focus on seeking God and His wisdom will be added to you. It is simple. And simplicity is what God seeks: *"the simplicity that is in Christ"* (2 Cor. 11:3) and *"simplicity of heart"* (Acts 2:46). Listen to what Paul writes to the Corinthians: *"...We conducted ourselves in the world in simplicity and godly sincerity, not with fleshly wisdom but by the grace of God..."* (2 Cor. 1:12). He instructs the Romans to *"be wise in what is good, and simple concerning evil"* (Rom. 16:19). In other words, wisdom requires you to be simpleminded regarding what is evil—your mindset about it needs to be like a child's, very black and white. Remember, *"...Not many wise according to the flesh, not many mighty, not many noble, are called"* (1 Cor. 1:26).

In Chapter 3, I showed you how the political spirit is crafty and cunning. Likewise, King Herod was sly and astute in his dealings with Jesus, and this craftiness proved to be his downfall. Worldly wisdom will be put to shame for *"God has chosen the foolish things of the world to put to shame the wise..."* (1 Cor. 1:27). God used what seemed to be foolishness to confound the wisdom of Herod.

Even though this spirit was in operation, Jesus, through the wisdom of God, conquered and defeated it. If He hadn't won, you and I wouldn't be saved today.

The whole time the Herodian spirit was trying kill Jesus, God—through His wisdom—used Herod to transition Jesus into fulfilling prophecy and destiny. So, even though this spirit was in operation, Jesus, through the wisdom of God, conquered and defeated it. If He hadn't won, you and I wouldn't be saved today. God's wisdom is the means to overcoming the craftiness of this the political spirit. No other wisdom will succeed at outsmarting this fox.

God's wisdom is the means to overcoming the craftiness of this the political spirit.

Look at Proverbs 24:3,5-6:

Through wisdom a house is built,
And by understanding it is established....

A wise man is strong,
Yes, a man of knowledge increases strength;

For by wise counsel you will wage your own war,
And in a multitude of counselors there is safety.

You don't war against flesh and blood. You war against principalities, powers, and rulers of wickedness in high places (Eph. 6:12). How do you that? With the wisdom of God—by wise counsel—you wage war.

Isaiah 11:2 states, *"The Spirit of the Lord shall rest upon Him, the Spirit of wisdom and understanding, the Spirit of counsel and might, the Spirit of knowledge and of the fear of the Lord."* When you have the spirit of wisdom, counsel, and might, you will be in a position to overcome the political spirit. How can you access and harness that wisdom? By abiding in Christ. You inherited the mind of Christ when you gave your life to Him. You exchanged your human wisdom for God's wisdom when you exchanged your heart of stone for one of flesh. *"You are in Christ Jesus, who became for us wisdom from God..."* (1 Cor. 1:30).

The Power of Hidden Wisdom

The most powerful weapons are the secret truths that God reveals to your heart. The revelation God gives you can be compared to the most high tech stealth missile that hits its target with laser-guided accuracy. Until it is activated and launched, it's hidden. It takes the enemy unaware. It remains concealed until the appointed time. God, in His wisdom, is the Master of covert operations. His wisdom is hidden from the enemy, and sometimes He even keeps His wisdom hidden from you. You must be willing to seek it out, dig for it, go farther, and look deeper into His heart as well as your own. *"You desire truth in the inward parts, **and in the hidden part You will make me to know wisdom"** (Ps. 51:6).

God is in the business of helping you grow. He is always working to increase your faith—as well as your faithfulness. Dealing with the sacred things of God requires discretion. You have to respect the power contained within the hidden wisdom of God, just as you would respect the powerful force of a missile. You cannot be careless when it comes to handling God's wisdom any more than you would be cavalier in dealing with the lethal weapons of modern warfare.

The Book of Proverbs says that where there is wisdom, there must also be discretion. *"...Keep sound wisdom and discretion; so they will be life to your soul and grace to your neck"* (Prov. 3:21-22). *"I, wisdom, dwell with prudence, and find out knowledge and discretion"* (Prov. 8:12). Discretion means that you don't reveal certain things until the appointed time. Paul wrote in First Corinthians 4:1 that, as the servants of Christ, we are the stewards of the mysteries of God. There is a reason that God keeps His wisdom hidden—but at the same time, in all *"wisdom and prudence,"* God had faith enough in us that He *"made known to us the mystery of His will"* (Eph. 1:8-9). We must therefore be faithful, *"as those entrusted with the secret things of God"* (1 Cor. 4:1 NIV).

Wisdom that is hidden is a mystery that has been concealed for an appointed time.

So what is this *hidden wisdom* all about? Wisdom that is hidden is a mystery that has been concealed for an appointed time. *"We speak the wisdom of God in a mystery, the hidden wisdom which God ordained before the ages for our glory"* (1 Cor. 2:7). There are mysteries concerning your life. There were also hidden mysteries concerning the life of Jesus so that, while He was alive on the earth, He continually pressed into the Spirit of God for the wisdom that He needed each day. At one point, we are told, in Luke 9:29-31, that while Jesus prayed He was transfigured and was given knowledge about His impending death: *"...The appearance of His face was altered, and His robe became white and glistening. And behold, two men talked with Him, who were Moses and Elijah, who appeared in glory and spoke of His decease which He was about to accomplish at Jerusalem."*

In the same way, we must press into the Spirit and pray for the wisdom that we need to accomplish what God has called us to do. *"For there is nothing hidden which will not be revealed, nor has anything been kept secret but that it should come to light"* (Mark 4:22). If you hope to find it, you must seek it out with your whole heart.

Yes, if you cry out for discernment,
And lift up your voice for understanding,

If you seek her as silver,
And search for her as for hidden treasures;

Then you will understand the fear of the Lord,
And find the knowledge of God (Proverbs 2:3-5).

Wisdom comes to us in stages. When you cultivate the knowledge that you have and observe correctly the wisdom that God gives you—when you begin to actively receive and walk in it—then God will give you more. Jesus taught this principle in Mark 4:23-24: *"If anyone has ears to hear, let him hear. Then He said to them, 'Take heed what you hear. With the same measure you use, it will be measured to you; and to you who hear, more will be given.'"* So when the Spirit of God begins to reveal knowledge about your situation, be diligent to walk in the counsel that He gives you.

When the Spirit of God begins to reveal knowledge about your situation, be diligent to walk in the counsel that He gives you.

You begin to access wisdom by walking in the fear of the Lord. In Psalms and Proverbs, we are told that divine wisdom begins with the fear of God. Isaiah prophesied that the Spirit of the fear of the Lord would rest upon Jesus, accompanied by the Spirit of wisdom and understanding (see Isa. 11:2). You must have a genuine fear, reverence, and honor for God in order to walk in His ways. Ask the Lord to show and reveal the fear of the Lord to you. It will cause you to hate evil. It will keep you safe from snares and traps. *"The fear of the Lord is a fountain of life, to turn one away from the snares of death"* (Prov. 14:27). In that place of godly fear, wisdom begins to come.

There is a reason that God requires you to fear Him if you are to access His wisdom. Wisdom is holy and precious; it is a treasure that you are being entrusted with to steward. You and I have been given *"...the knowledge of the mystery of God...in whom are hidden all the treasures of wisdom..."* (Col. 2:2-3). Solomon wrote in Proverbs that wisdom is more valuable than precious metals or gemstones. *"How much better to get wisdom than gold..."* (Prov. 16:16).

> *Receive my instruction, and not silver,*
> *And knowledge rather than choice gold;*
>
> *For wisdom is better than rubies,*
> *And all the things one may desire cannot be compared*
> *with her* (Proverbs 8:10-11).

Proverbs 8 also tells us that whoever loves wisdom will inherit wealth.

> *My fruit is better than gold, yes, than fine gold,*
> *And my revenue than choice silver.*
>
> *I traverse the way of righteousness,*
> *In the midst of the paths of justice,*
>
> *That I may cause those who love me to inherit wealth,*
> *That I may fill their treasuries* (Proverbs 8:19-21).

The fruit of wisdom is better than gold, and she will fill your treasuries with true riches. But notice where wisdom is found: in the way of righteousness. When your heart is upright before the Lord because you honor and reverence Him—in that place of godly fear you will find all of the wisdom that you need to bind the strong man and plunder his goods.

If you ask, God will give you wisdom and unveil hidden mysteries concerning your assignment. That is what God's Kingdom life is all about. But it is also about learning to trust God with what you don't know and what He doesn't show you. You may get a general sense of the overall direction that He is moving you in but not have clarity regarding every detail. God will reveal what you need to know when you need it in order to fulfill your assignment. That is the key to discernment—it is the sense of *what* you need to do in the moment rather than *why*. I am actually now comfortable not knowing what is going on all of the time. I am totally fine with God not telling me everything. In fact, I'm on "one-word notice." All I need to know is what I am supposed to do in the present moment.

God will only reveal as much wisdom as you need to hear and obey. You can have knowledge about something and not heed it. We have all fallen victim to not fully walking in the truth that we know. You may know that junk food is bad for you and still eat it—or that too much sun is dangerous and still get a sun burn—but if you are to grow in the wisdom of God, you must be willing to act on what He shows you. Wisdom comes with doing what you know to do. The more you practice doing what God shows you to do, the more wisdom you will be given.

> **Wisdom comes with doing what you know to do. The more you practice doing what God shows you to do, the more wisdom you will be given.**

This is why the fear of the Lord in the beginning of wisdom (see Prov. 9:10). It is the fear of God that compels us to obey Him. Wisdom requires obedience. The disobedient are likened to fools in the Bible. Whenever we do not heed the wisdom that we have been given, we are being foolish. If we are to receive instruction from the Lord and to grow in wisdom, then we must grow in our ability to hear *and* obey Him.

Once you find the confidence to obey whatever you hear God tell you to do, you will see His hand come upon you. His will is that you would go from glory to glory as you become more like Jesus. As you behold His glory—His wisdom—you become a reflection of that glory and wisdom. You *"are being transformed into the same image from glory to glory, just as by the Spirit of the Lord"* (2 Cor. 3:18). Your inheritance in Christ is the glory of God. He is preparing and posturing you to walk in a measure of glory that you have not yet seen. Wisdom will always precede His glory, and glory will always reveal wisdom. It's a cycle. They go together, the glory and the wisdom of God. *"The wise shall inherit glory..."* (Prov. 3:35).

Get a hold of God's wisdom—*"do not be vague and thoughtless and foolish, but understanding and firmly grasping what the will of the Lord is"* (Eph. 5:17 AMP)—*"gird up the loins of your mind..."* (1 Pet. 1:13)—and then rest in the knowledge of Him *"that your faith should not be in the wisdom of men but in the power of God"* (1 Cor. 2:5).

Meditation Points

- How did the first apostles gain victory over the political spirit working through Herod—and how will the Church gain victory over the same spirit still opposing Christ today? Pray for God's particular strategies and action plan for you and your church community.

- How can you safeguard yourself against being drawn in by human or demonic wisdom?

- Did you recognize how the wisdom of God took the political spirit and the enemies of Jesus in their own craftiness causing Jesus to fulfill His assignment on the cross?

- How can you make way for God to reign as sovereign over your enemy's plots and plans?

- What is your plan for fathoming the hidden wisdom of God? Are you ready to dedicate the time necessary to find and operate in it?

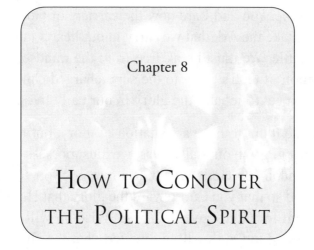

Chapter 8

HOW TO CONQUER
THE POLITICAL SPIRIT

*They saw that the wisdom of God was in him, to
do what is right and fair* (1 Kings 3:28 NLV).

*We speak the wisdom of God in a mystery,
the hidden wisdom which God ordained before
the ages for our glory* (1 Corinthians 2:7).

Wisdom not only prepares a platform for you to experience
God's glory, but it also increases your capacity to convey it. In
other words, as you grow in the wisdom and knowledge of God,
you will be capable of carrying God's glory into the circumstances of your life. The day is coming when God's people will
become the containers of glory that they were created to be and
will bring it to the people who need to be touched by it most. As
David's heart was to transport the Ark of the Covenant back into
the midst of God's people, (1 Chron. 13:3) so should the heart of

the Church be. You and I are now the carriers of God's covenant and should take the Ark that we carry in our hearts into the midst of every battle. We must break free from the mindset that limits the visitation of God's glory to the supercharged church service. We must expect to inhabit the glory in our daily lives.

It is one thing to have a visitation of glory, but to carry and steward that glory in our daily lives, we must possess some of the deepest wisdom of God. Wisdom empowers you to know the ways of God so that you can steward the glory that He brings into any situation for God's given purpose. Wisdom will attune your heart and mind to God's will, no matter what the circumstances. Wisdom will enable you to harness the glory that you need to overcome your enemy.

Wisdom is the principal thing;
Therefore get wisdom.
And in all your getting, get understanding.

Exalt her, and she will promote you;
She will bring you honor, when you embrace her.

She will place on your head an ornament of grace;
A crown of glory she will deliver to you (Proverbs 4:7-9).

Wisdom always precedes glory. When you operate on behalf of the wisdom of God, the glory of God operates on your behalf. You are making a way for the glory of God to reign in that situation. As the steward of a vineyard, you don't *make* the vines grow, but you prepare an environment where they are nurtured and protected and can flourish. You make room for the natural process of growth to take place unencumbered. When it comes to the work of the Spirit, you make way and *give place* to the Lord—you make room for the glory of God to operate unhindered.

Jesus operated in wisdom and made room for God to operate sovereignly on His behalf. Jesus did not confront the political spirit head-on, knowing that God ultimately *"...catches the wise in their own craftiness"* (Job 5:13). He bided His time. He waited for God to order His steps. He was patient and discerning about when to step out and when to step back, about when to speak and when not to speak. Whenever you are confronted with the political spirit, God will deal with it for you. It is not in your power to overcome it by force, but when you submit to God, what appears to be working against you will mysteriously begin to work in your favor.

> **Whenever you are confronted with the political spirit, God will deal with it for you. It is not in your power to overcome it by force, but when you submit to God, what appears to be working against you will mysteriously begin to work in your favor.**

This is what you see happen in the story of Esther. Esther dealt with the political spirit operating against the seed of Jacob through a politician named Haman. Haman is a self-promoting demagogue who hates Mordecai, Esther's uncle and a respected Jew, because he refuses to bow down and pay homage to him. Haman refrains from taking action against him personally because he fears popular opinion. Instead, he sways the public—and the king—to take action against all Jews throughout the kingdom on the premise that *"...their laws are different from all other peo-ple's, and they do not keep the king's laws. Therefore it is not fit-ting for the king to let them remain"* (Esther 3:8). The word *demagogue* is defined as "a political leader who seeks support by appealing to popular passions and prejudices,"¹ and that is what Haman does. He convinces the king that Jews are disloyal and provokes the people to covet the Jews' possessions.

> *Dispatches were sent by swift messengers into all the provinces of the empire, giving the order that all Jews— young and old, including women and children—must be killed, slaughtered, and annihilated on a single day. This was scheduled to happen on March 7 of the next year. The property of the Jews would be given to those who killed them* (Esther 3:13 NLT).

The alliance that Haman makes with the king appears cata-strophic for the Jewish people. In the natural, Haman has all the power, with the backing of the king and the law on his side. The situation looks hopeless. Yet God's hidden wisdom is at work. Yes, the Jews fast and pray. Esther bravely approaches the king seeking his favor, but does not yet make her appeal known. She has prepared a beautiful banquet, only to request that the king and Haman return again the next evening. That night, Haman, full of wine and his own importance, erects a gallows on which to hang Mordecai. And that night, the king cannot sleep and asks to read the book of records. The king discovers how Mordecai has faithfully served him and inquires of Haman how he might honor one so faithful. Instead of hanging him on the gallows the next day, Haman has to parade Mordecai about the city wearing the king's robes upon the king's horse proclaiming, *"Thus shall it be done to the man whom the king delights to honor"* (Esther

6:9). While you are trying to make sense of everything, God is at work on your behalf doing above and beyond what you could ask or imagine (see Eph. 3:20).

> **While you are trying to make sense of everything, God is at work on your behalf doing above and beyond what you could ask or imagine.**

That day, when the king and Haman return to Esther's banquet, she makes her petition known. Note that it is the king who inquires what he can do on her behalf. The king asks what her request is, and Esther responds by requesting the lives of her people. Esther has wisdom, which means that she also has discretion. She has enough discretion to hold back and to not speak to the king until the appointed time. That takes character.

Do you know it takes more character to *not* say something than it does to say it? Because she waits, the king comes to know and honor Mordecai, and when he finds out that Haman has planned to kill him, the king is furious. He has Haman hung on the same gallows that he planned for Mordecai. The king gives Mordecai Haman's house and his signet ring to decree with it whatever he wills. So Mordecai sends a letter on the king's authority decreeing that the Jews can kill anyone who attempts to do them harm. When the appointed day comes, the Jews kill all of their enemies and gain the upper hand throughout the land.

And all the officials of the provinces, the satraps, the governors, and all those doing the king's work, helped the Jews, because the fear of Mordecai fell upon them. For Mordecai was great in the king's palace, and his fame spread throughout all the provinces; for this man Mordecai became increasingly prominent. Thus the Jews defeated all their enemies with the stroke of the sword, with slaughter and destruction, and did what they pleased with those who hated them (Esther 9:3-5).

Because Esther operates with the wisdom of God, the glory of God prevails. She is prudent and discreet and earns the favor of the king. Likewise, Mordecai is exalted because of his honor and faithfulness. Both respect the authority of the king while at the same time fearing God, and through prayer and fasting, they are able to follow God's lead. They make room for God to work on their behalf, and the enemy is destroyed.

Discretion and Honor

Part of stewarding the wisdom of God is learning to hold your tongue. I know how difficult that can be because I have carried things in the spirit and have not been allowed to tell anyone. If you have ever been pregnant, you know how hard it is to not tell someone about it. You may be nine months pregnant in the spirit, bulging to the point that you want to burst. People are asking you what you are pregnant with, but can't tell them. That is because the word—or wisdom—in you is for a season. You must keep it to yourself, cultivate it, and let it grow to term. David wrote, *"...In the hidden part You will make me to know wisdom"* (Ps. 51:6). God's word is perfected in you while it is yet hidden.

When you are pregnant with a word, you have to steward the mystery while it matures in your spirit until the appointed time.

God's word is perfected in you while it is yet hidden.

Mark 4:17 states that *"...persecution arises for the word's sake...."* What word? The word you are carrying within you—the hidden wisdom you are carrying in the womb of your spirit. You might not even be aware of it yet, but it is there. The wisdom hidden within you will bring about persecution and affliction because you are pregnant with something that is not just about you. When you give birth to that word, it will bring life to everyone around you. The enemy knows that, so persecution and affliction come—but all the while, your baby is still growing.

I have learned over the years that, when I am pregnant with the word, opposition comes. The word I'm carrying is a hidden mystery that has been unveiled to me. What is revelation? It is hidden wisdom, revealed. What is hidden wisdom? Revelation concealed.

Hidden wisdom has been stored up for our glory. Paul says, *"We speak the wisdom of God in a mystery, the hidden wisdom which God ordained...for our glory"* (1 Cor. 2:7). There are mysteries concerning your life and mine. When God reveals something to your heart, keep it, meditate on it, study, and pray about it. There will be a season during which the revelation that God gives you will need to mature in your spirit. You steward the word

God plants in your heart much like an expecting mother would carry a baby growing within her.

There are mysteries concerning your life and mine. When God reveals something to your heart, keep it, meditate on it, study, and pray about it.

When a mother is expecting, certain things change in her life. She can't eat certain things, do certain things, or be exposed to certain things for the sake of the baby. Certain habits and associations have to change. When God impregnates you with revelation, then you have to separate yourself far beyond normal. It is not just about you, but it is about what you are carrying and stewarding. It is about what you are expecting.

That is why you must walk in love, even when you are being mistreated. Your baby is too important for you to go to war—you don't want to lose your baby prematurely. That is what Jesus did in Matthew 14 when Herod killed John the Baptist. When Jesus finds out, He disappears. He goes to another place. He does not want to take on Herod at that time because He knows that an appointed time is coming when He will be called to face him. He wasn't there to die at Herod's hand; He was there to give His life for you and me according to the will of the Father.

Jesus knew that there was a plan in place. In John chapter 2, when Jesus is at a wedding and they run out of wine, Jesus says, *"...My hour has not yet come"* (John 2:4), but He goes ahead and turns the water into wine for those who are present. Jesus rarely says anything that is just about that moment. There is always a prophetic depth underlying His remarks. When He speaks of His hour not yet having come, He means His hour to die on the cross, which would be followed by pouring out the Holy Spirit and the new wine of His glory on all of humanity. The living water of His life would be turned into the new wine of the Spirit made available for all.

Jesus speaks that way because He is focused and discerning. Solomon writes in Ecclesiastes 8:5, *"...A wise man's heart discerns both time and judgment."* In John 4, the disciples see Jesus talking to a woman at the well. After He ministers to her, she leaves her water pot and disappears. They ask Him if He would like to eat. He answers, *"I have food to eat of which you do not know"* (John 4:31-32). He is in a different world. They don't understand Him. They look at one another and ask, *"Has anyone brought Him anything to eat?"* But Jesus says, *"My food is to do the will of Him who sent Me, and to finish His work"* (John 4:33-34). What is He talking about? When Jesus sees the woman at the well, He sees the harvest. He gets caught up in it. That is why He is there—for the nations. He tells His disciples, *"...Lift up your eyes and look at the fields, for they are already white for harvest"* (John 4:35).

Information will never impregnate you. Revelation will.

There is a season when you are pregnant and nobody knows about it. But then a time comes when you can't hide it anymore. It is just like that in the spirit. You are pregnant in the womb of your spirit by revelation knowledge, not by information. Information will never impregnate you. Revelation will. When you are in the chamber of His glory and the Holy Spirit impregnates you with revelation knowledge, then, wrapped in the seed of God's word, revelation knowledge begins to spring up in your spirit, and you begin to carry life. You carry the word conceived within you like Mary carried the Word within her womb—only she carried the literal Word of God made flesh. You carry the word that God gives you to bring life and deliverance within the womb of your spirit.

God has prepared your spirit to carry the word—the hidden wisdom—that is a mystery until you give birth to it. In the birthing process, you become one with that word. As you carry it and fellowship with it, you will get to know the word of deliverance that you are carrying. You will begin to see the power of it. And when it is time, the world will be ready to receive it.

Bringing Forth the Promise

When the season comes for you to bring forth the word that God has planted in your heart, you will experience pressure. This is a time of transition. Just like when the baby is in the birth canal, you will be in a place where you think nothing is happening. Things don't seem to be moving, yet there is intense pressure. But as with natural birth, there is no turning back. The time is at hand, and the baby will be born.

When the word does come forth, you have to pay even more attention because satan will come immediately to destroy it. Be on your guard and don't lose heart. Herod tried to destroy Jesus in his infancy and had all the babies in Bethlehem killed in the process. Jesus—the Word by which everything was created—had to flee to Egypt. But the day came when He took on Herod. The very thing the enemy was using to destroy God's plan helped to forward it.

You are always pregnant with something new that you never knew was possible. It is something that is not the norm for you. It will challenge you and cause you to step out of your comfort zone. You will wonder if you can really do it. But it is God who is at work in you—*"He who has begun a good work in you will complete it..."* (Phil. 1:6).

Many of you are forerunners. The opposition, circumstances, and the pressure that you are facing means that you are contending for something that you are pioneering. Something new is about to be born, though it is not new to God. It might not even be new to other people. But to you it is definitely new. There is tension within your spirit because change is taking place. You can't take the pressure personally. When you are in that transition period, what do you do? You push. How do you push? You pray. That is the time for intercession and praying in the Spirit. During that time, you cannot rely on anything else but praying in the Spirit to bring the promise forth. The baby is just about out, and you need supernatural assistance.

Something new is about to be born.

God is raising up people in churches as midwives. A midwife anointing is being released so that pastors and leaders can help people give birth supernaturally to the things of God. This is where wisdom and discretion come in. If someone else is excited and they are in their birthing season, you bless and support them. Are you willing to help other people give birth to their babies when you are pregnant with twins, or triplets, or quadruplets? Are you willing to lay down your life for others when you are "heavy with child"?

Proverbs 17:8 says, *"A present is a precious stone in the eyes of its possessor...."* Other people's babies are just as important as yours, but yours is especially important in your eyes. To all of us, our gifts look great, but at the end of the day, they are no different to God. The measure of grace is given according to the gift, so God gives us each a unique grace just as we have a special grace for our own natural children—yet in the eyes of God, all are equally valuable.

Whatever God has graced you with, value it, nurture it, and bring it to fruition. As Paul tells Timothy, *"Do not neglect the gift that is in you..."* (1 Tim. 4:14). If you are pregnant with a baby, with a ministry, with a task, you have to give birth to it. If you have not felt new life stir within you for a while, allow the presence and the glory of God to revive it, and then pray for wisdom to carry it. If you have miscarried in the past, learn from it and carry the next one to full term. I've lost a couple of babies in the spirit, and that is why I want to help you understand how to give birth to the promise that God has given you. However you have failed before, or whatever you have felt you've lost in the spirit, God will restore it and create in its place something fresh and new.

Wisdom and understanding will help you and preserve you. As Solomon writes, *"Wisdom is a defense..."* (Eccles. 7:12). Wisdom is as much a defense as it is a weapon of war.

When wisdom enters your heart,
And knowledge is pleasant to your soul,

Discretion will preserve you;
Understanding will keep you,

To deliver you from the way of evil (Proverbs 2:10-12).

Learning how to carry the living word is important. That is wisdom. That is what Jesus did. He had a destiny. He didn't speak of it all the time. He said, *"I have food to eat of which you do not know."* Most of the time, His disciples didn't understand what He was talking about until long after it had come to pass.

You may be asking, "Lord when is it going to happen. Is it *ever* going to happen?" Be open to where God is showing you to be obedient, and then align your life. Also remember that, *"To everything there is a season, a time for every purpose under heaven"* (Eccles. 3:1). He appoints a delivery date that you don't know of. When you are just ready to give birth, and you feel like everything that you have done has failed you, God will say, "No My child, it hasn't. I need you to obey Me just for who I Am, not for what it would bring you in your life." God is longing for you to obey Him because of who He is and because He spoke to you as a father. *"My son, attend to my words; consent and submit to my sayings"* (Prov. 4:20 AMP).

When you hear those words, God is saying, "Listen. The time is just about here."

When you hear those words, God is saying, "Listen. The time is just about here." Then you will know that it is time to let go and to let God bring the promise forth. It is God who makes it happen. It is God who manifests His wisdom and glory through you. It is God who works through that wisdom to bring down strongholds. It is God's presence that breaks every yoke. It is God who will accomplish all things on your behalf.

When you are stewarding the wisdom and glory of God, you have to remember who you are carrying it and speaking it for. Be ever mindful that you do it all to the glory and praise of God. That is how the walls of Jericho came tumbling down, and that is how the enemy's governmental strongholds in these last days will crumble (see Josh. 6:1-5). As the Body of Christ, individually and corporately, increases its capacity to contain and carry the honor and glory of God, the enemy will not be able to stand against it.

When you go through these stages in your life, always remember that it is all about bringing glory to God. You should remain in the state where "your keys are always hanging out." My keys are always available. As long as my keys are available to God, He lets me hold them. The minute I make them mine, it doesn't work anymore. Every step of the way, I ask, "Father, do You want Your keys back? Do You want me to walk away from my dream, the vision You birthed in me, the passion You placed in me? Do You want me to lay the promise You gave me on the altar?" When you are able to do this, then you will see His hand move.

Meditation Points

- How can you cultivate discretion in your life? Can you keep a secret? Study the word *discretion* in the Book of Proverbs, and ask God to show you how you can develop it in your life.

- What is God impregnating your spirit with? How are you caring for and nurturing that word? What changes do you need to make as you spend time with God and in the world?

- God wants you to learn to steward His secrets for a season. How can you do that?

Endnote

1. *Collins Essential English Dictionary*, 2nd edition, s.v., "Demagogue."

Chapter 9

MAKE WAY
FOR THE GLORY

*I will shake all nations, so that the treasures
of all nations shall come in, and I will fill
this house with glory, says the Lord of
hosts....The latter glory of this house shall
be greater than the former, says the Lord of
hosts. And in this place I will give peace,
declares the Lord of hosts* (Haggai 2:7,9 ESV).

God is building His temple—and He will fill it with His glory. It is only by the glory of God that the strong man working against the government of God will be bound. And that glory resides in you—*"what are the riches of the glory...which is Christ in you, the hope of glory"* (Col. 1:27). When believers come together with one accord—in the unity of the Spirit and in the bond of peace—that glory will tear down every enemy stronghold; but that glory must be harnessed corporately through the living temple that is Christ's Body. Though we are each individually *"the temple of the Holy Spirit"* (1 Cor. 6:19), we are also collectively the house of God, which God is building up and furnishing with *"the treasures of all nations."*

God is building His temple brick by brick by bringing His purpose to pass in each of our individual lives. The temple of God must be built according to God's standard—every stone in its proper place—and that is why it is so important that you and I line our lives up with His righteousness. That is why God must expose the false governing systems in our churches and denominations; only then can God's house be erected in truth and wisdom and be able to bear the weight of His glory.

> *Behold, the Man whose name is the Branch!*
> *From His place He shall branch out,*
> *And He shall build the temple of the Lord;*
> *Yes, He shall build the temple of the Lord.*
>
> *He shall bear the glory,*
> *And shall sit and rule on His throne;*
> *So He shall be a priest on His throne,*
> *And the counsel of peace shall be between them both*
> (Zechariah 6:12-13).

We are the living temple of the Lord within which Christ sits as King and Priest. We have talked about the unrighteous alliance that exists between these two offices—the political and religious—yet here we see this alliance embodied and perfected in Christ. The Amplified Bible's version of Zechariah 6:13 reads: *"...And the counsel of peace shall be between the two [offices—Priest and King]."* When God's government is established, there will be perfect harmony between these two roles. Jesus will rule as King and serve as Priest. This represents true servant leadership and the kind of leadership that we should strive to emulate. The authority that we have been given in Christ to reign as kings is first and foremost to serve as priests—interceding and advocating on behalf of the lost.

As one of the living stones that God is using to build His temple, you have been created with a unique purpose. That purpose is ingrained in the fiber of your being, as are the various minerals that form a rock. As with a stone, your composition was foreordained before the foundation of the earth. You may endure intense heat and pressure, but that doesn't change the signature of your composition. You were created with a unique purpose and brought to the surface; perhaps through a series of upheavals or relentless erosion, you emerged at this particular point in the earth's history for a reason.

When you get a revelation of how special and on purpose you are, you will begin to glimpse the extent of God's love toward you.

When you get a revelation of how special and on purpose you are, you will begin to glimpse the extent of God's love toward you. He loves you so much that He sent His Son to die on the cross so that He could have fellowship with you. And that fellowship is so much more important to Him than your purpose—because you being reconciled to Him is the ultimate purpose for it all. At the same time, there is no greater joy than knowing that you are "on assignment" and no greater satisfaction than fulfilling it. That assignment, in one way or another, will involve preparing the way—preparing hearts to receive more of God's glory. That is what aligning our lives does. That is why we are to be led by the Holy Spirit, to walk in love, and to *"put on the new man which was created according to God, in true righteousness and holiness"* (Eph. 4:24).

This is how we position our hearts to receive the glory of God. The glory of God is His love—His substance. There is purpose for His glory. When we talk about alignment, really we're talking about what John the Baptist and Jesus preached, *"The time is fulfilled, and the kingdom of God is at hand. Repent, and believe in the gospel"* (Mark 1:15). And later when Jesus sent His disciples two by two, *"they went out and preached that people should repent"* (Mark 6:12). And then, after Jesus had ascended to the right hand of the Father, Peter urged the people, *"Repent therefore and be converted, that your sins may be blotted out, so that times of refreshing may come from the presence of the Lord"* (Acts 3:19).

Corporate Repentance

We need to come to a place of deep repentance in our hearts. We need to clear a path and repair the breaches—to unclutter the streams of living water. There should not be any blockages in your relationship with God. You cannot afford to compromise in your walk with Jesus. When He speaks to your heart and asks you to do something, you should have clarity about doing it without hesitation. When the Lord asks you to make those little adjustments—to hold your tongue, to check your attitude, or take every thought captive to the obedience of

Christ—there should be no compromise or ambiguity about what to do.

Joyful are those who obey His laws and search for Him with all their hearts.

They do not compromise with evil, and they walk only in His paths (Psalm 119:2-3 NLT).

That is the place we need to be, individually as well as corporately. This is what God is doing now in the Body in regards to leadership. For the next generation, leaders must be completely open before God and completely transparent before the people. Even with our mistakes, in humility, we must say, "Yes, I've made these mistakes; forgive me and help me to change, Lord." I have been through a lot of dark times in my life and have made many mistakes, but I can always turn to God and ask for His forgiveness. It is still true today that, *"If we confess our sins, He is faithful and just to forgive us our sins and to cleanse us from all unrighteousness"* (1 John 1:9).

That is where the manifestation of His glory has come in my life. I have been at rock bottom and seen His glory. I have been in the pit and cried out to God and discovered that in the lowest places is where I've had the most significant encounters with the glory of God. *"I dwell in the high and holy place, with him who has a contrite and humble spirit, to revive the spirit of the humble, and to revive the heart of the contrite ones"* (Isa. 57:15). There is a purpose for His glory. God is in the business of reviving, restoring, and healing broken hearts. God wants your whole heart to be complete and intact, united to fear His name so that you can walk in His truth (see Ps. 86:11).

God is in the business of reviving, restoring, and healing broken hearts. God wants your whole heart to be complete and intact, united to fear His name so that you can walk in His truth.

Now, corporately there is a call for the Church to humble herself so that God's glory might dwell within her. God has been bringing alignment individually because He is preparing us corporately to move forward as an army to receive and convey His glory. As a container, together, we are going to open our hearts to walk in the *"fullness of Him who fills all in all"* (Eph. 1:23).

We will no longer stay where we were, but we will come up in the Spirit. This why alignment is so important—don't be offended or put off because God is continually bringing your life into deeper alignment. One gentleman said to me, "I'm done with the pruning in my life. I'm finished with it. I don't want any more pruning. I've been going through it for so long that I am done with it."

I said, "Brother, until we see that manifestation, until we see those veils lifted and removed so that we can see Jesus face-to-face, there will be pruning!"

We are not to compromise in this season. We are touching a realm of such supernatural faith that, when God tells us to do something, we will say "yes" without wavering. We will trust God with our finances, our families, and our future. There will be a new level of faith and grace. So many things are happening in the Spirit, as well as in the natural. Denominational barriers are coming down. Systems of man are coming down. We will start to see a unity in the Spirit. We are seeing this in some of the Muslim nations where believers get together and worship and the glory of God is there. This is how they can live in a hostile nation where they know that the next time they step out the door they might be killed. They are able to live every single day confident that God is preserving them.

When the western Church gets a sense of destiny and purpose beyond providing the most high-tech multimedia church services—when we get a hold of the fact that our lives have a global and eternal purpose—we will walk in the level of unity required to do warfare. Mind you, I think that high-tech excellence is awesome and that media is an amazingly relevant tool for our age, but let's not forget the eternal purposes of God along the way. We must go beyond this to begin to prepare the way for greater glory that will expel the thick darkness at work in the world. We must be willing to ask the Lord how we can align ourselves with what He is doing corporately—and then be willing to hear and obey what He says. Otherwise, we will be like those God warned through the prophet Jeremiah, *"...I spoke to you, rising up early and speaking, but you did not hear, and I called you, but you did not answer"* (Jer. 7:13).

We must keep our hearts transparent before God and one another. We must be quick to confess our sins to one another and to ask God for forgiveness. If we aren't especially circumspect during these times of upheaval, we could give the enemy a foothold and lose significant territory. We would do well to heed Hosea 11:5: *"...The Assyrian shall be his king, because they refused to repent."*

The Cost of Compromise

Compromise can unravel even the most called and anointed of leaders. The wisest, most prosperous king ever to rule Israel was undone by neglecting to obey God in one area. King Solomon learned the hard way that *"a little leaven leavens the whole lump"* (Gal. 5:9). He went on to write in the Book of Ecclesiastes, *"Dead flies putrefy the perfumer's ointment, and cause it to give off a foul odor; so does a little folly to one respected for wisdom and honor"* (Eccles. 10:1). Solomon personally experiences the perfumer's ointment being fouled when he disobeys God and irrevocably compromises his legacy. In First Kings, we read what happens to Solomon—one greatly respected for wisdom and honor—as a result of "a little folly:"

> *But King Solomon loved many foreign women, as well as the daughter of Pharaoh: women of the Moabites, Ammonites, Edomites, Sidonians, and Hittites—from the nations of whom the Lord had said to the children of Israel, "You shall not intermarry with them, nor they with you. Surely they will turn away your hearts after their gods." Solomon clung to these in love* (1 Kings 11:1-2).

God asked Solomon not to be affiliated with these women or to enter into covenant with them. Even in this season, God is asking us not to enter into certain alliances. There are business associations that can look advantageous, but they will spoil your anointing as the fly spoiled the ointment. If God is calling you to a higher place with Him, He will ask you to sanctify yourself. You may be in that place where God is asking you not to make certain alliances with specific people or organizations so that you won't be derailed later on. There might not be anything wrong with them, but God knows when it is better for you not to be allied with certain folks—lest they *"turn away your heart."* Sometimes He calls you to stand alone because that is what will keep you close to Him. God deals with us individually for the good of our souls as well as for the eternal purpose that He has ordained for us.

In Solomon's case, God asked him specifically not to get involved with foreign women, yet he *"clung to these in love."* And we know from the next verse that he didn't just get involved with one or two but that he had *"seven hundred wives, princesses, and three hundred concubines,"* and as a result, *"his wives turned away his heart"* (1 Kings 11:3). Solomon compromised and *"did not fully follow the Lord, as did his father David"* (1 Kings 11:6). At the end of the day, he lost everything. God told Solomon, *"Because you have done this, and have not kept My covenant and My statutes, which I have commanded you, I will surely tear the kingdom away from you"* (1 Kings 11:11).

This is what happens with alliances. In the present moment, they appear profitable, but when you are yoked with another, you will inevitably be pulled in the direction that they are going.

This was the cost of compromise. These women turned Solomon's heart. *"...His wives turned his heart after other gods..."* (1 Kings 11:4). This is what happens with alliances. In the present moment, they appear profitable, but when you are yoked with another, you will inevitably be pulled in the direction that they are going. That is why God wants your life to be aligned with His will—so that some little alliance will not cause you to pursue a false objective and cost you and your descendants God's best future.

David, on the other hand, had a heart after God's heart—even though he made some mistakes. Compromise, therefore, is a condition of the heart. David stumbled, but his heart always turned back toward God. For David's sake, God held back a remnant of the kingdom: *"I will not tear away the whole kingdom; I will give one tribe to your son for the sake of My servant David, and for the sake of Jerusalem which I have chosen"* (1 Kings 11:13).

So where was the compromise? It was in Solomon's alliance with idol worshipers. What was the consequence? *"The Lord raised up an adversary against Solomon, Hadad the Edomite; he was a descendant of the king of Edom"* (1 Kings 11:14).

This is a perfect illustration of the season that the Church is in now. God is asking His people to separate themselves. Pay attention to the alliances that you make in your personal and professional life. Guard your heart, not just for your own sake, but also for the sake of the generations to come. Do not dishonor your commitments or those in authority over you, but make sure that you steer clear of any unholy alliances. Make sure that your heart is turned toward God and aligned with what He is calling you to do.

God is doing something in the Body of Christ. The kingdoms and systems of man are crumbling. Leaders have been challenged because God is calling them up higher. We need to be praying for those in leadership. Pray that God would give leaders the spirit of repentance. Pray that the Church throughout North America would submit to the will of God and repent. God has a critical assignment for the Church of the United States, Canada, and the western world. We are on a threshold, and if we don't get serious about turning our hearts back toward God, we will miss out on the *kairos* opportunity that is at hand to take territory for God's Kingdom.

God, in His mercy, is calling for repentance in our nations, churches, and denominations. He is raising up a generation of leaders whose hearts will turn toward Him and whose collective voice will be like one crying out in the wilderness, "Prepare the way!" Men and women from every arena will turn their faces back to God. They will humble themselves before the Lord and before the people. The Lord will give them a revelation for the generations to follow. We will all begin to sense the importance of the decisions that we make in light of the present Kingdom and of eternity.

Consecrate Yourself

God is calling His people up higher. He is asking His people to set themselves apart as Daniel did. *"Daniel purposed in his heart that he would not defile himself with the portion of the king's delicacies, nor with the wine which he drank..."* (Dan. 1:8). Daniel and his three kinsmen chose not to partake of the king's meat, and *"...God gave them knowledge and skill in all literature and wisdom; and Daniel had understanding in all visions and dreams"* (Dan. 1:17). This is a representation of what is happening on a spiritual level right now. God is bringing those of you with businesses into a place where you will need to purpose in your heart not to operate according to the world's ways.

Entrepreneurs and business leaders must make the decision not to "eat of the king's meat"—in other words, not participate in the way that the world takes care of business.

With this stand will come blessing, but the political spirit will also try to strike you down through the jealousy and envy of others, just as it attacked Daniel later in his life. When he was young, Daniel's friends faced the fiery furnace because of their stand, but God stood with them and they were delivered (see Dan. 3). Years later, Daniel is a chief advisor to King Darius, and the other advisors and governors grow jealous of him because of the favor that he has with the king and his position in the government. Seeking to find something to accuse Daniel of, they convince the king to pass a law against appealing to anyone but the king for 30 days. Thus, when Daniel prays, he can be held in violation of that law. Anyone who breaks this law will be thrown into the lions' den (see Dan. 6). It was an extreme form of office politics, but is not that different from what many Christians experience every day where they work and go to church, though they experience it to a much lesser degree.

Notice the work of the political spirit in this. It used envy and jealousy to inspire a legalistic attack on righteousness to keep God's blessings from flowing through the counsel and wisdom of Daniel. However, because Daniel is firmly seated in his position of authority and refuses to act unrighteously, the hand of God moves on his account and stays the mouths of the lions. When Daniel emerges unscathed, his accusers are tossed into the den in his place. Daniel's enemies are destroyed in the same trap they had set for him, just as Haman was hung on the same gallows that he had erected to execute Mordecai.

What I want you to see is that people who do not compromise when facing the political spirit will be promoted and transitioned out of their season of preparation and into their place of destiny. God will always turn the tables on your enemies and take the wise in their own craftiness. When you refuse to compromise, and when you stay true to your divine assignment, then God will overcome the "wise," who are assembled against you, in their own plots, and He will position you in a higher seat of authority under His sovereign hand.

> **I believe entrepreneurs will prosper as never before when they choose to conduct their affairs in the same way that Daniel chose to conduct himself in the king's palace.**

I believe entrepreneurs will prosper as never before when they choose to conduct their affairs in the same way that Daniel chose to conduct himself in the king's palace. If business people are equally mindful about remaining transparent and uncorrupted, about staying lean and sharp, then God will give them insight into new markets and creative products and services. He will give them profitable ideas that the marketplace has not yet seen or heard of. *"Eye has not seen, nor ear heard, nor have entered into the heart of man the things which God has prepared..."* (1 Cor. 2:9). God is going to release unprecedented innovations and discoveries so that *"in all matters of wisdom and understanding"* the market will find them *"ten times better"* than any other *"in all* [the] *realm"* (Dan. 1:20).

Finances will be made available from sources that we have never before considered; wealth will come forth out of dark places, not just symbolically, but also from places that have been hidden under the ground, natural and spiritual oil wells that will be released and opened up. This is the time when we must make the choice about whether to pursue the world or God. If we are to obtain the supernatural results that we know are possible, then we need to be spending more time in the prayer closet than anywhere else.

Friendship with the world can prove to be enmity with God (see James 4:4). We have to continually assess our motives and make certain that they are pure and righteous. We have to be sure that we are not compromising in our businesses, our ministries, our families, or in our personal lives. We have to come to a place where we can say, "God, I will not compromise. I will not allow myself to go down that route." Ask God to show you those things that you should prune from your life.

Many of you have wondered why God has asked you to not go to certain places or do certain things. You may have felt like you've been suppressed, but actually God has been keeping you from going down the wrong path. He has been holding you in a certain location because of a *kairos* season that is coming upon you. As we kick into that corporately, you will be released. It will seem as if the lid is lifted off as things begin to happen in your life. You will discover that you are able to pray for hours—going places in your prayer closet that you never thought possible. You will notice that you are positioning your heart with a greater degree of circumspection in order to more accurately line it up with the heart of God.

It will seem as if the lid is lifted off as things begin to happen in your life.

Corporately, there will be an increase of revelation. This is an era of the spirit of revelation. I was in a prayer meeting recently when we came to this place in the spirit where all of a sudden someone said, "God is telling me that we don't have the understanding of the Word. God wants to take us higher, but there is not the understanding right now." The Spirit of God will increasingly compel us to fast and pray and to pull ourselves back so that we can dig deeper in the Word. In doing so, we will get new spiritual insight and revelation that will enable us to walk in greater authority. I am not talking about revelation that has already been released, but brand new revelation that we will begin to walk in corporately.

We are coming up in the spirit. No longer will you be able to get by only showing up for church on Sunday, but God will call you to walk more intimately with Him every moment of every day. The King of Glory is coming—and because the King of Glory is on His way, He will release His glory in the midst of those whom He finds worshiping Him in spirit and truth.

Lift up your heads, O you gates!
And be lifted up, you everlasting doors!
And the King of glory shall come in (Psalm 24:7).

If we want to partake of this glory, then we have to be prepared as a people. As a people, we must repent, refuse to compromise, press into the Word, sanctify our hearts, and consecrate our lives. It could be that we are called to repent for the sins of past generations—sins that we don't even know about because they have been hidden. God is bringing everything to the surface, but we need to pray that God gives repentance to the nations and to the leadership of North America.

Character Testing

This is an exciting time. We seriously need to rise up in the spirit and pray for our leaders. We have to come to a place where we are clear and free of any negative view of authority. Our ability to submit to, pray for, and bless those that God places in authority over us has a great deal to do with the glory that we will experience. Where there is dissention, there is strife and every evil thing. If we don't align our hearts with those whom God places in authority, then the unity required to bring forth God's glory will not be present. If you are to be the vessel of honor that Paul writes to Timothy about (see 2 Tim. 2:21), you must be in one accord with your leaders. Your attitude toward those whom God's gives authority over you is a clear demonstration of your character.

Before *"the kindness and the love of God our Savior toward man appeared"* (Titus 3:4), Paul writes to Titus, *"we ourselves were also once foolish, disobedient, deceived, serving various lusts and pleasures, living in malice and envy, hateful and hating one another"* (Titus 3:3). But now that we have been made the righteousness of God in Christ, Paul exhorts Titus to *"remind them to be subject to rulers and authorities, to obey, to be ready for every good work, to speak evil of no one, to be peaceable, gentle, showing all humility to all men"* (Titus 3:1-2). This is what godly character looks like. Those whose hearts are pure, whose motives are righteous, will walk in the wisdom of God which is *"first pure, then peaceable, gentle, willing to yield, full of mercy and good fruits, without partiality and without hypocrisy"* (James 3:17).

I have great dreams for the glory of God. I've experienced some things in His glory, but there is much more that I want to experience. I know that I will, but I also know that I can't make it happen by sheer force of will. There will be a testing of character—defining moments that will determine whether or not I walk in that glory. Every patriarch in the Bible was faced with a defining moment in his life. Abraham was asked to submit his desire—his dream—and to sacrifice the most precious thing that God gave Him. He laid his own agenda on the altar, and as a result, God used it to establish His covenant of peace with all of humanity (see Gen. 22:15-18).

That is what defined Abraham as the father of faith. He was willing to submit to God's authority and to place his dream on the altar, knowing that God would keep His Word and resurrect it. He fully believed that God would raise Isaac from the dead. In his heart, Abraham allowed God to crucify Isaac—and because he did, God allowed His own Son to be crucified. Just as with Abraham, God will take you to a moment in time when the direction of your life will be determined by a single decision.

The more you step into the center of His will, the more you will have faith to obey those inner promptings—and the more you step into the unknown, the more you will step under the sovereign hand of God.

—— 201 ——

The more you step into the center of His will, the more you will have faith to obey those inner promptings—and the more you step into the unknown, the more you will step under the sovereign hand of God. Remember that the corporate hand of God is very different from His personal hand and Spirit upon you. God's corporate hand moves season to season. God's corporate hand is not just about you and me, but it is about His hand over what He is doing across the Body.

God's hand might be over here in one season, and then in the next season, it might move over there. You have to come under that hand. You have to have faith to obey and follow Him. That is why people miss it. In one era, they discern the cloud. Then the cloud moves, yet they stay. They had a true experience of God's glory in one season, but in the next, it becomes a barrier between them and their future. That is why God desires to train you to live by what you have not known, not by what you have known. What you *don't know* is actually greater than what you *do know* (see Ps. 51:6).

When I was a Muslim, what I didn't know was greater than what I did know—and that was the realization of who Jesus Christ is. I came to a revelation of Him as the Son of God. Then I realized that, in my present reality, there were other things that I did not know. I knew Jesus, but I didn't know that through Jesus I could have insight into my purpose and destiny. Then God began to reveal mysteries concerning my calling and made known to me aspects of His hidden wisdom.

In November 2002, I was in my bedroom praying, and the Lord spoke to me. He said, "My son, get in my Word and prepare yourself because I am going to open doors for you to share My Word, reveal My mysteries, and preach My gospel in this nation and in the whole world." That word has not been totally fulfilled, but the first fruits of it have been. We are on various television networks already—and God opened every door. It didn't look like it was going to happen, but then it did! It happened slowly, but every step was exciting. Who made it happen? Not me. I have never asked for a meeting. I have never pursued a single contact. People ask me, "How does this work for you?" I say, "I have a contact." They say, "Yeah, you have to have contacts! Who is it?" I say, "I have the Father! He's my only contact!" It's not about what you know; it is about Who you know. And it's not about impressing the masses; it's about playing to an audience of One.

Quiet Confidence

Why would you want to live this life if you have to fight all the time? If you think that you have to be your own savior and be at war (left, right, center, up, and down), watching for everything—the political spirit, the Jezebel spirit, and the religious spirit—it can completely wear you down! But when you know that God's hand is coming on you for your assignment, you can rest in that. The hand of the Lord will preserve you so that you learn to have confidence in Him.

Who you are in Christ will begin to emerge. Who you are speaks volumes to the enemy. You've heard the story of the sons of Sceva. They wanted to use the technique that Paul used to cast devils out of people. But the devil said, "Excuse me, I know who Jesus is. I know who Paul is. But who are you?"

Do you understand what it means to take on the name of Christ? The sons of Sceva used His name, but they didn't know

Him. They did not know who they were in Him. The devil then said, "I don't know who you are either" (see Acts 19:13-16).

> **Faith will give you a victory over an event. But love will make you more than a conqueror.**

In contrast, when confronted by Jesus, demons say, "We know who you are. You are the son of the Most High" (see Mark 5:7). That is part of dealing with the devil. Grace will get you through a problem. Faith will give you a victory over an event. But love will make you more than a conqueror. Love is not so much something that you do as something that you are. When you realize who you are, you will understand your authority as a king and priest because that is who God made you to be. You can look in the face of terror because you know who He is in you. You know who He has made you to be because of His great love, and you can, therefore, stand in the midst of opposition. That is how you stand strong. Your identity emerges as you embrace His love working for, in, and through you.

Get that boldness into your heart. Then you will live from a different realm. You won't live on the outside trying to make things happen. You will enter a place of rest. This is how Jesus managed to sleep on the boat in the midst of a storm (see Mark 4:38). This is how you fight in the spirit. The highest form of spiritual warfare is resting in the knowledge that God's presence is with you at all times and is undergirding every circumstance. You must get into that place of rest where you have a knowing—where you know what God said and so you position yourself under that Word. You must see God's provision in your mind's eye. You must have expectation. When the enemy comes against you and sees the hand of the Lord, he will flee in terror.

I don't want to do anything without the hand of the Lord hovering over me. I get nervous if I don't see His hand. When I know that His hand is upon me, I will step out into potentially dangerous situations, confident of the Lord's presence and guidance. If my heart is turned toward Him—or upright before Him—I can rest knowing that He will back me up. *"...Your righteousness shall go before you; the glory of the Lord shall be your rear guard"* (Isa. 58:8). If you keep your heart, God will keep you. In Romans 12:19, He said, *"Vengeance is Mine."* In this verse, He also said, *"give place to* [My] *wrath."* How do you give place to the wrath of God? You move out of the way. Forgive and release the person or the situation as fast as possible. Guard your heart by keeping it clear of envy, strife, and unforgiveness. These are all footholds that the political spirit will use to manipulate you and to make you protective of your position or jurisdiction. This is a primary stronghold that the political spirit will build in your life, and before you know it, you will be doing things that you never intended to do in order to keep what you think is yours. The Spirit of God works completely differently—He works to promote others and to get out of the way when someone else needs to come in for a task that will further the Kingdom of God. Like Barnabas, we need to get out of the way when God is promoting someone else. It is not about being the top person, but about setting the stage for the glory of God to manifest and operate freely.

Keep your heart with all diligence, and God will back you because, in so doing, He is backing His eternal purposes. He lines you up with your purpose to the degree that you are able to get a hold of who you are in Him. He works on your behalf to the extent that you give place to His Spirit and His will. Establish in your heart *who* you belong to and allow Him to mold you into that image. Remember that your identity always precedes your purpose. If you seek to know your purpose before you know your identity, your purpose will become your identity. If you build your life on the gift, your gift will become an idol and keep you from the God who gave it to you.

Don't forget that who you are is more important than what you are called to do. When you get a revelation of your identity in Christ and allow His identity to emerge through you, you will have victory over any Herodian or political spirit. The strong man will have no power over you.

Nothing can prevail against that love because it is the wellspring of wisdom.

Love is the expression of Christ in you. Nothing can prevail against that love because it is the wellspring of wisdom. Nothing can touch the wisdom that God gives you as you walk in His love—because that wisdom always springs forth from love. When you operate out of the love of God, it unleashes God's glory and disarms the enemy.

In order to expose the false, we must raise the banner of Truth—individually and collectively. Individuals determine the integrity of governing systems—and motives of the heart determine the integrity of individuals. If the Church is to establish God's divine order, every member of the Body must keep their motives pure. Guard your heart. Check your motives. Bring every thought captive to the obedience of love, because love conquers all. Then watch what God does—this is only the beginning of the adventure, not the end goal!

Meditation Points

- How was Jesus the perfect king and priest? How does His example teach us to operate in the authority that God wants to bestow upon us?

- How are you keeping your heart pure before God so that you can fulfill your assignment? Do you need a time of repentance? Are you checking your motives to keep them aligned with God's plumb line? Are you allowing the husbandman to work in your life, pruning that which is unhealthy so that you can produce more fruit?

- Who else are you joining with to accomplish the corporate mission of the Body of Christ in your area? Are you on the same page with one another and the Spirit of God regarding what needs to be done? Are there alliances that you have made that are harmful and need to be severed?

- Are you ready for God to turn the tables on your enemies like He did for Daniel?

- Remember, it is God who will take the wise in their own craftiness, not you.

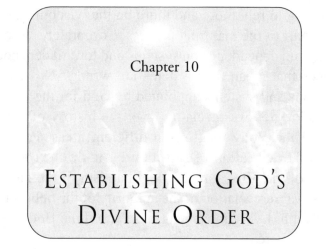

Chapter 10

ESTABLISHING GOD'S DIVINE ORDER

For unto us a Child is born,
Unto us a Son is given;
And the government will be upon His shoulder.
And His name will be called
Wonderful, Counselor, Mighty God,
Everlasting Father, Prince of Peace (Isaiah 9:6).

Systems are changing. God is revealing His wisdom in order to establish His divine order. We are entering a season when human systems will become increasingly dependent upon God's sovereign rule. As in the Old Testament, under David, Solomon, and Jehoshaphat, leaders will become unashamedly reliant on God's direction. They will turn to their prayer closets to seek God's wisdom; they will seek the counsel of prophets for confirmation. As the Church matures, she will become increasingly dependent on hearing the voice of God.

Learning to rely more and more on the wisdom and counsel of God is part of the maturing process. Corporately, we are moving away from dependence on systems and toward dependence on God. Does that mean that systems are wrong? No. There have been seasons and systems appointed by God for the maturing of the Body. Progressive revelation over the history of the Church has helped the Body to grow in different areas. For example, there was the revelation of salvation by faith; then there was a revelation of the gifts, tongues, and baptism of the Holy Spirit; then there was a revelation of the authority of the believer and the power of faith. Every movement has caused the Body to mature in a particular area.

God is building His temple floor by floor. Every Church era represents a floor—or level—that has been built on the original foundation. From generation to generation, specific revelations have come forth for the purpose of framing the next floor of the temple. We need to take the revelation that we have been given and continue to build—we need to pass the baton to the next generation, leaving a legacy that allows them to continue building.

Pressing Forward

Corporately, we are now in a season of global alignment. The floor that we are building will be laid on the revelation that we have received regarding divine order. God has dropped His plumb line into the midst of His Church and is aligning His people according to His purposes. He is raising the banner of truth to which we must align our hearts. *"You have given a banner to those who fear You, that it may be displayed because of the truth"* (Ps. 60:4)—the wisdom of God is the banner that will be revealed by those who fear the Lord. Alignment will only be possible when the Spirit of the fear of God rests upon the Church.

God is establishing His government on the shoulders of the Body of Christ. In the Old Testament, in order for the priests to carry the Ark of the Covenant upon their shoulders, divine order had to be established. In the New Testament, the priests are the body of believers among—and within—whom God is establishing His Kingdom; we are coming into alignment *"as one body and one spirit"* upon whose shoulders His government can rest (see Eph. 4:3-6). When this happens, the Spirit of the Lord shall also rest upon the Church, *"the Spirit of wisdom and understanding, the Spirit of counsel and might, the Spirit of knowledge and of the fear of the Lord"* (Isa. 11:2).

As we align our lives to God's sovereign rule, His divine government will begin to manifest.

As we align our lives to God's sovereign rule, His divine government will begin to manifest. However, in order for there to be alignment, there must first be a fear of God—and in order to operate in *"the spirit of knowledge and the fear of the Lord,"* we must be willing to look in the mirror of His Word and face the reflection of both the goodness and severity of His glory. We need to value the awesome comfort of the Holy Spirit as well as experience the weighty reverence and fear of the Lord. After all, *"our God is a consuming fire"* (Heb. 12:29).

As we have seen, with God's glory comes a revelation of His exceeding goodness, but also a revelation of His judgment. *"I will set My glory among the nations; all the nations shall see My judgment..."* (Ezek. 39:21). As we spend time in the Word of God, we will behold *"as in a mirror the glory of the Lord,"* and we will be *"transformed into that same image from glory to glory"* (2 Cor. 3:18). His righteousness is established as each of us works out our *"own salvation with fear and trembling"* (Phil. 2:12). How do you work out your own salvation with fear and trembling? You humble yourself, you reverence the Holy Spirit, and you don't take God's Word lightly.

God says, through Isaiah, *"...I will look to the one who has no pride and is broken in spirit, and who shakes with fear at My Word"* (Isa. 66:2 NLV). Paul writes to the Corinthians, *"His [Titus'] affections are greater for you as he remembers the obedience of you all, how with fear and trembling you received him"* (2 Cor. 7:15). And James writes, *"...Receive with meekness the implanted word, which is able to save your souls"* (James 1:21). Jesus says of the person who rejects Him, *"...The word that I have spoken will judge him"* (John 12:48). The Word is living. It discerns and judges the motives of the heart:

> *For the word of God is living and powerful, and sharper than any two-edged sword, piercing even to the division of soul and spirit, and of joints and marrow, and is a discerner of the thoughts and intents of the heart* (Hebrews 4:12).

What makes the Word living and powerful? The Holy Spirit. *"For our gospel did not come to you in word only, but also in power, and in the Holy Spirit..."* (1 Thess. 1:5). The Word and the

Spirit work together to produce the fruit of righteousness in your life. The Book of Ephesians tells us that the Word of God is the sword of the Spirit (see Eph. 6:17) and that, having believed the Word of truth, *"you were sealed with the Holy Spirit of promise"* (Eph. 1:13). As the Word takes up residence in your heart, so will the Holy Spirit.

The Holy Spirit takes up residence in your spirit to enable you to reflect God's glory. Your body is the outer court; your soul is the inner court, and the holy of holies is your spirit—and this is where the Holy Spirit dwells. In the Old Testament, God's Spirit was veiled in the temple behind the curtain that covered the holy of holies. When Christ made the final sacrifice upon the cross, the curtain was torn from top to bottom (see Matt. 27:51). Through tradition, many in the Church have veiled the Spirit of glory on the inside of their spirits—they have not given Him access to come forth and reveal Himself in wisdom, in power, and in God's glory. As the temple of the Holy Spirit—individually and corporately—we must behold the glory of God *"with unveiled face"* so that the Spirit of God can transform us to reveal that same image (see 2 Cor. 3:18).

> **As the temple of the Holy Spirit—individually and corporately—we must behold the glory of God *"with unveiled face"* so that the Spirit of God can transform us to reveal that same image (see 2 Cor. 3:18).**

When we *"behold [in the Word of God] as in a mirror the glory of the Lord..."* (2 Cor. 3:18 AMP), we are seeing the glory of God at work in us reflected back. We are to be the visible image of God's glory. An *image* is something visible. It is a representation or likeness of something otherwise invisible. Jesus was the express image of God the Father—*"the brightness of His glory and the express image of His person..."* (Heb. 1:3)—in order to show the world the true nature and character of God. Likewise, we are to be the image-bearers of Jesus—the visible expression of an invisible God. As Jesus revealed the Father, you and I are to reveal Jesus.

As you gaze into the mirror of the Word, you will begin to see Christ formed in you—your *"hope of glory"* (Col. 1:27). James talks about looking into the mirror of the Word to see what kind of person you are, *"like a man observing his natural face in a mirror"* (James 1:23), but Paul talks about looking into the mirror and beholding the glory of God. In this mirror, you get past yourself and begin to look at Jesus. You begin to look at the Spirit of God that is placed within you. As the reflection of Christ is formed in you, you begin to see the Father.

First John 3:2 says that when we see Him, we shall be like Him—and that *"everyone who has this hope in Him purifies himself."* Why does this hope purify you? Because you will ultimately become what you see. If you see Jesus, you will become like Jesus. Through this process of looking in the mirror and beholding His glory, you are transformed. You will see your strengths and success in Christ rather than your faults and failures. Who you are without Him diminishes—and who you are in Him emerges.

As you press into the Word, you will begin to reflect the glory of God. When Moses came down from the mountain after receiving the terms of the covenant, his face *radiated* with the glory of God (see Exod. 34:29 NLT). Being in God's presence and fellowshipping with His Word caused Moses' face to *shine forth with beams* of God's glory (see Exod. 34:29 AMP). Moses aligned Himself with the Word of God by immersing Himself in the presence of God. As your life becomes increasingly aligned with God's Word, you will progressively reflect more of His glory—and you will be positioned for God to release His authority through your very presence. As you reflect God's glory and goodness, God's government will begin to reign, and the false governing systems built on deceit and corruption will be dismantled.

No one person can advance God's Kingdom all by himself or herself. The more of us who are aligning our lives to the plumb line of God's Word, *"from a pure heart, from a good conscience, and from sincere faith"* (1 Timothy 1:5), and who are positioned in our places of authority in our unique callings, the more effectively the Kingdom of God can advance and be established corporately. Your capacity to be a vessel of God's glory by walking in the fullness of your divine calling is about God's sovereign hand coming into operation to fulfill what was ordained before the foundation of the world. This capacity is in the DNA of who you are; it is in the blueprint of your spirit man. God wants His glory to be manifested in the natural world *through you*. He prophetically ordained that the government would rest on the shoulders of the Body of Christ—His Church; for every believer *"...is the image and [reflected] glory of God [his function of government reflects the majesty of the divine Rule]..."* (1 Cor. 11:7 AMP).

Removing the Leaven

The political spirit is the spirit of false government. It always rears its head when the true government of God is about to be established. In Mark 8:15, Jesus warns his disciples saying, *"Beware of the leaven of Herod and the leaven of the Pharisees."* When put into dough, a little leaven expands rapidly and *"...leavens the whole lump"* (see Gal. 5:9). That is why the Israelites had to remove all of the leaven from their homes before the Passover could be celebrated (see Lev. 23:6). In the same way, we need to remove the leaven from the Church, the leaven of impure motives; for the false intentions of even a few have a corporate impact on the Body of believers. Paul tells the Corinthians to *"...purge out the old leaven, that you may be a new lump, since you truly are unleavened. For indeed Christ, our Passover, was sacrificed for us"* (1 Cor. 5:7).

In the same way, we need to remove the leaven from the Church, the leaven of impure motives; for the false intentions of even a few have a corporate impact on the Body of believers.

Paul exhorts the Corinthians to conduct themselves not *"...with the leaven of malice and wickedness, but with the unleavened bread of sincerity and truth"* (1 Cor. 5:8). Removing the leaven requires honesty and transparency. For this reason, God is exposing hidden agendas in this hour.

> *...He will both bring to light the secret things that are [now hidden] in darkness and disclose and expose the [secret] aims (motives and purposes) of hearts. Then every man will receive his [due] commendation from God* (1 Corinthians 4:5 AMP).

This is why it is imperative that the Spirit of the fear of the Lord comes upon the Church! More than ever, God is sounding the alarm: *"Awake, you who sleep! Arise from the dead! And Christ will give you light"* (Eph. 5:14)—because it is only the light of Christ that can reveal truth and dispel the deceptive forces of darkness.

Paul tells the Ephesians:

You were once darkness, but now you are light in the Lord.... Have no fellowship with the unfruitful works of darkness, but rather expose them. ...But all things that are exposed are made manifest by the light, for whatever makes manifest is light (Ephesians 5:8,11,13).

There is a battle taking place between the true and the false—between the light and the dark—a spiritual battle that is determined by every decision you make. Each time you compromise the truth for a convenient falsehood, the leaven of Herod expands the lines of darkness and God's Kingdom loses ground. Joel says it well when he prophesies, *"Multitudes, multitudes in the valley of decision! For the day of the Lord is near in the valley of decision"* (Joel 3:14).

Before God's Kingdom is established, God's people will have to pass through the valley of decision. They will have to make some choices about who they will serve. Joshua 24:14-15 commands God's people to *"fear the Lord, serve Him in sincerity and in truth.... Choose for yourselves this day whom you will serve...."* Will you align yourself with the systems of Man or of God? The enemy will not make the choice easy. Before God's government is established among the living on the earth, the political spirit will attempt to turn the hearts and minds of the people of God.

The political spirit is the leaven of Herod—the leaven of political deception that attempts to establish its rule before the sovereign rule of God takes hold. The leaven begins to ferment through envy, which leads to strife, and quickly expands into widespread corruption. It idolizes human reasoning and intellectualism. Paul tells Timothy how to recognize those governed by such a spirit:

> *He is proud, knowing nothing, but is obsessed with disputes and arguments over words, from which come envy, strife, reviling, evil suspicions, useless wranglings of men of corrupt minds and destitute of the truth, who suppose that godliness is a means of gain. From such withdraw yourself* (1 Timothy 6:4-5).

Paul then gives Timothy the antidote, instructing him:

> *Flee these things and pursue righteousness, godliness, faith, love, patience, gentleness....Guard what was committed to your trust, avoiding the profane and idle babblings and contradictions of what is falsely called knowledge* (1 Timothy 6:11,20).

True knowledge is what has been committed to Timothy's trust. Knowledge of the truth is what saves and empowers us. *"His divine power has given to us all things that pertain to life and godliness, **through the knowledge of Him**..."* (2 Pet. 1:3). Paul prays that the *"Father of glory"* will give us *"**the spirit of** *wisdom and revelation in the knowledge of Him"* (Eph. 1:17). Knowledge of God will give you the wisdom and revelation that you need to overcome the schemes of the enemy.

Those who have a true knowledge of God have a true fear of God. You will read in Proverbs 15:33 that *"the fear of the Lord is the instruction of wisdom."* Those who fear God will operate in the wisdom needed to bring alignment to the Body of Christ; that alignment will cause truth and justice to shine forth into every dark corner. Isaiah 33:6 states, *"Wisdom and knowledge will be the stability of your times..."*—it will bring protection and provision to the Church—the same verse in the New International Version adds *"the fear of the Lord is the key to this treasure."*

The fear of the Lord brings blessing and deliverance, for those who fear the Lord have nothing else to fear. When you have a reverence and awe for the majesty of God, you will begin to see God expose and exterminate your enemies. The fear of Lord protects you because it causes you to guard your heart. When you fear God, you *"guard your heart with all vigilance"*—which is of critical importance for victory because out of your heart *"flow the springs of life"* (Prov. 4:23 AMP). The fear of the Lord preserves your heart because it does not allow bitterness, anger, resentment, offense, or unforgiveness to clutter the springs of living water coming forth from your spirit—which would ultimately contaminate the well of wisdom hidden within you. Again, Proverbs 14:27 states, *"The fear of the Lord is a fountain of life, to turn one away from the snares of death."* And in Proverbs 16:6, we read: *"In mercy and truth atonement is provided for iniquity; and by the fear of the Lord one departs from evil."* The fear of the Lord will keep the motives of your heart pure.

In the same way that heat neutralizes yeast, the fear of God neutralizes the leaven of Herod.

In the same way that heat neutralizes yeast, the fear of God neutralizes the leaven of Herod. The fear of God will keep you from falling into temptation and will deliver you from evil. In Isaiah 31:9, we read that the Lord, *"whose fire is in Zion and whose furnace is in Jerusalem,"* says, *"He shall cross over to his stronghold for fear."* Fear will cause the Lord's *"prisoners of hope"* to *"return to the stronghold"* of their salvation (Zech. 9:12).

The fear of God is an *"all-consuming fire"* that burns away the chafe from our lives. In Exodus 24:17, we read, *"The sight of the glory of the Lord was like a consuming fire...."* The glory of God is a fire that destroys every sinful intention. If you are to withstand the fire of the glory of God, you must purge the leaven of malice and envy from your heart—*"laying aside all malice, all deceit, hypocrisy, envy, and all evil speaking"* (1 Pet. 2:1).

"...Who can survive this all-consuming fire?"
Those who are honest and fair,
who refuse to profit by fraud,
who stay far away from bribes,
who refuse to listen to those who plot murder,
who shut their eyes to all enticement to do wrong—"
(Isaiah 33:14-15 NLT).

The Goodness and Severity of God

Romans 11:22 says, *"Consider the goodness and severity of God...."* Too often we look at the goodness and mercy of God, but neglect the fear of God. In this season, I see the Lord bringing the fear of God back into the Church. The next move of God will be preceded by a fear of the Lord because God is bringing purity. Walking in purity, justice, truth, and righteousness is the only way to overcome the spiritual forces of darkness. God's people will wage battle in this way:

By purity, by knowledge, by longsuffering, by kindness, by the Holy Spirit, by sincere love, by the word of truth, by the power of God, by the armor of righteousness on the right hand and on the left (2 Corinthians 6:6-7).

Paul tells the Corinthians that they are only restricted by their *"own affections"* (2 Cor. 6:12). When fear of the severity of God is present, God's people will choose to walk in the ways of God rather than their own.

In Acts 9:31, we read, *"The churches...had peace and were edified. And walking in the fear of the Lord and in the comfort of the Holy Spirit, they were multiplied."* The fear of God brought the comfort of the Holy Spirit. The fear of the Lord is a fountain of life because it allows you to cut through the garbage of your mind and to tap into the clear springs of life emanating from the wellspring of your spirit. To wage spiritual battle, you need to have the ability to override the voice of your soul and to tune into the voice of your spirit. The Word of God is the tuning fork that you use to accurately discern the voice of the Spirit of truth.

Hebrews 4:12 says that we must allow the Word of God to divide between soul and spirit, between the thoughts of our minds and the intentions of our hearts, between marrow and bone: *"The word of God is living and powerful...piercing even to the division of soul and spirit, and of joints and marrow...."* That is a prophetic symbol; marrow refers to the spirit man and bone refers to the soul. Jeremiah says, *"...His word was in my heart like a burning fire shut up in my bones..."* (Jer. 20:9). Jeremiah is speaking about a passion that rises from the life of that word in his spirit, from the fountain of life within him. This life comes forward, causing him to declare, "I can't help but make mention of his name! I can't help but walk in the path that God has ordained for me! I can't help but speak forth that which God has placed in my heart."

His intention is that we would see through the smokescreens of the enemy's distractions, human agendas, and our own natural desires, in order to take hold of His will.

When we are battling forces that operate through deception, we can have the best intentions and still be deceived. Through God's goodness, He allows His severity to bring alignment in order to protect us. His intention is that we would see through the smokescreens of the enemy's distractions, human agendas, and our own natural desires, in order to take hold of His will. We are often blinded to God's wisdom and His divine order. Paul writes, *"Do not be unwise, but understand what the will of the Lord is"*

(Eph. 5:17). David has the best intentions when he desires to bring the Ark of the Covenant back to Jerusalem, yet, because he does not understand God's divine order, people were hurt (1 Chron. 13:10). Ultimately, God's severity in dealing with Uzza saves David and all of Israel.

Before God brings His glory, He will bring alignment. Divine order always precedes God's glory. David has a heart and passion to see the glory of God. After Uzza is struck dead for mishandling the Ark, David takes it to Obed-Edom, who was a Levitical priest. While the Ark remains with Obed-Edom, everyone is blessed—yet when they attempt to carry it on their own, people die. What was the difference? It is the same Ark. It is the same glory. It is the same God. In one place, it produces blessing; in another place, it produces judgment.

Yet, even in judgment, there is mercy. If that fire had not consumed Uzza, God's wrath would have fallen on every single one of them in Jerusalem, including David. They were doing something that was not according to God's divine order, and it needed to be stopped. First Chronicles 15:13 states, *"The Lord our God broke out against us, because we did not consult Him about the proper order."* What was the divine order that they were not following? It had to do with who was handling the Ark. Only the Levites were authorized to transport the Ark. Not just anyone could put the Ark on their shoulders and carry it, no matter how well intentioned they were. God's divine order dictated that only the priesthood could handle the holy things of God. That was the divine order established in the Old Covenant. In the New Covenant, we are all called to be a royal priesthood by Jesus who *"made us a kingdom of priests for God His Father"* (Rev. 1:6 NLT).

Your spirit, indwelt by the Holy Spirit, is infused with all knowledge and wisdom— but your soul must continually be renewed.

So how does this apply in a practical sense? It applies to your ability to differentiate between the voice of your soul and your spirit. The fountain of life that gives direction springs forth from your spirit to keep you from *"the snares of death."* Your spirit, indwelt by the Holy Spirit, is infused with all knowledge and wisdom—but your soul must continually be renewed. It is what you must continually work to save with *"fear and trembling"*—yielding it to God's will and purposes (see Phil. 2:12). Sometimes it is as if your mind has a mind of its own!

In Psalm 13:2, David cries out to the Lord, *"How long shall I take counsel in my soul, having sorrow in my heart daily? How long will my enemy be exalted over me?"* This is what we have to watch out for. There is danger when we take counsel from our souls, especially when our souls are in an emotional state of crisis. It doesn't matter whether it is anger, unforgiveness, bitterness, hurt, pain, or turmoil. Whatever the situation or issue, it will throw you off course. If you take counsel from your soul, you risk obscuring the voice of God because it will be filtered through your emotions. There is a very thin line—a thin veil—between your soul and your spirit—and that veil can cloud God's wisdom. God is teaching His people to discern the voice of their spirits, removing the veil so that they can get wisdom straight from the heart of God.

When you are led by your soul, the Spirit of God is not leading you. You could be led astray by feelings or some crisis that happened in your life. Every time you come across that crisis again, you will respond out of fear, insecurity, or perhaps even jealousy. Proverbs 16:25 observes, *"There is a way that seems right to a man, but its end is the way of death."* We have to come to a place of maturity where our counsel is coming from the Spirit of God. It is a learning process. Every trial and temptation is an opportunity to learn how to be led by the Spirit of God, who resides in your spirit. Allow Him to transform your soul.

The Kingdom of God Within You

Where does divine order exist today? It exists in the Scriptures, and it exists in your spirit. How does it exist in your spirit? God says that, in the New Covenant, He will write His Word and His laws on your heart. God speaks through Ezekiel saying, *"...I will take out your stony, stubborn heart and give you a tender, responsive heart"* (Ezek. 36:26 NLT). He goes further, promising that He will cause you to obey Him.

> *I will give you a new heart and put a new spirit within you; I will take the heart of stone out of your flesh and give you a heart of flesh. I will put My Spirit within you **and cause you to walk in My statutes, and you will keep My judgments and do them*** (Ezekiel 36:26-27).

Paul writes to the Corinthians, *"Clearly you are an epistle of Christ...written not with ink but by the Spirit of the living God, not on tablets of stone but on tablets of flesh, that is, of the heart"*

(2 Cor. 3:3). Paul also writes to the Philippians to *"...work hard to show the results of your salvation, obeying God with deep reverence and fear. For God is working in you, giving you the desire and the power to do what pleases Him"* (Phil. 2:12-13 NLT). How does God give you the power to do what pleases Him? Through the fear of the Lord. When the fear of the Lord comes, it causes us to walk in His ways.

When we take counsel from our flesh, our soul, our emotions, or our situations, it is counsel based on circumstances (circumstantial evidence) and is usually rooted in fear of something in the world rather than in faith—in self-preservation rather than love. God has given us a new paradigm. Under the New Covenant, we have been born of the Spirit of God and are regenerated. He has given us a brand new spirit, and He has invited us to come and meditate on the Scriptures to allow His Word to dwell in and govern our hearts. *"Your word I have hidden in my heart, that I might not sin against You"* (Ps. 119:11). God wants you to take counsel from His Spirit that is alive in His Word.

It is not an overnight process. You start by meditating on His Word. His Word will put a dividing line between your soul and your spirit and allow you to differentiate between the thoughts of your heart and the thoughts of your mind. A very small percentage of professing Christians ever read the Bible. An even smaller percentage study and meditate upon the Word of God every day. Without the Word of Truth ruling in your heart, the Spirit of Truth will not reign, and the Spirit of knowledge, the fear of the Lord will be absent.

God's government is established through people. He chooses to rule and reign through people, and He puts people in places of authority. He gives them governmental authority and backs that governmental authority when they speak. This is what happened in the apostle Paul's life. As long as he was on assignment and speaking on behalf of the government of God, God backed him.

God's divine rule is being established as a sword right through His Church.

The age that we are moving into is the establishment of the government of God's Kingdom. Certain things that you could get by with during the previous age, you can no longer continue to do in this new era. This is because God's divine rule is being established as a sword right through His Church. This is not for personal benefit, but for the benefit of all humankind. It's about God's desire for all the people.

If God's government is not in place, the political spirit will continue to deceive and corrupt. The strong man must be dealt with from a governmental perspective. God is calling men and women to step into places of authority in their nations so that decisions and judgments can be made according to the government of God's Kingdom. When you are in a leadership position, remember that you are not there to fulfill your personal agenda. You are on assignment. It is not about what you want; it is about establishing God's government. When we represent the government of God, we are representing God Himself—and there are certain standards that God requires.

While God is working out things with us individually, He is also working out something corporately in His Church. We can't miss out on what God is doing! This is why God wants alignment individually and corporately—so that we will be attuned to His voice and in a position to walk in His authority.

The strong man in a nation will only be removed when the government of God is brought into order. Otherwise, that strong man becomes a governing spirit that holds sway over a city, region, or nation. When you go to certain countries, you will see this Herodian spirit alive and well in the earth today. The atrocities and turmoil throughout the continent of Africa are a result of the political spirit taking hold because true government has never been established. Decades of political alliances and deception have led to rampant corruption and strife—deadly political factions and tribal divisions that seem irreparable.

Most recently exposed in international news is "The Strong Man of Zimbabwe," Robert Mugabe, who has wreaked havoc in that country for 28 years. One of the most corrupt leaders on the continent, he ruthlessly manipulated, rigged, bullied, and bribed his way into power. He is just one living example of the evil men and impostors who *"will grow worse and worse, deceiving and being deceived"* (2 Tim. 3:13). Since he took control, the country has become one of the poorest in Africa. "Along with the devastated economy has come a dreadful human toll. Zimbabwe now has the world's lowest life expectancy—thirty-seven years for men, thirty-four for women—and about a quarter of its 12.5 million people are infected with the AIDS virus."[1] That is the cost to humanity when God's government is not firmly established and when the political spirit is left to have its way without interference from righteous people.

Like many other dictators who have risen to power, Mugabe began with good intentions. As a politically-minded young man, he sought to change his country for the better. He studied law and politics and learned how to advance himself and his agenda through the world's system. He sought independence for the former colony, and although he liberated the country from British rule, he and his country became enslaved to his desire for control. What brought out his dark side? Many believe that when Nelson Mandela supplanted him as Africa's most popular and enlightened leader, "Mugabe's jealousy drove him over the edge."[2]

This is an important lesson for the Church. We must be particularly mindful of envy working in the members of the Body. The Church won't be able to deal with this spirit in the harvest field until it is dealt with at home. *"For we ourselves were also once foolish, disobedient, deceived, serving various lusts and pleasures, living in malice and envy, hateful and hating one another"* (Titus 3:3). The political spirit looks for doorways—for human agendas and self-seeking motives—for footholds in the lives of individuals. The key to shutting the door to the political spirit is to keep your heart from envy. *"A sound heart is life to the body, but envy is rottenness to the bones"* (Prov. 14:30). You and I, and every member of the Body of Christ, must keep our motives pure before the Lord—free from motives tainted by personal, selfish agendas.

Before this spirit is overcome in the world, it must be overcome in the Church. Robert Mugabe, like Herod was, is consumed with protecting his position and maintaining his territorial authority. We must be very careful not to put our own territorial guards up within the Church. We must be like Barnabas rather than King Saul. When Saul saw his kingdom being passed to David because of his iniquity, he sought to kill him, and he did everything from slaughtering priests who aided David to going to soothsayers for advice (1 Sam. 28:7). Barnabas, however, when he discovered that he was going to go from being the man in charge to a follower of his own disciple, Paul, merely stepped aside so that God's Kingdom could advance. He saw that his reward was not in his position and authority within the early Church, but in following God with all of his heart. Through his humility, the Church was blessed and the Kingdom of God advanced like never before. We certainly need more Barnabases in the Church today.

> **The political spirit begins to operate within the Body because members...become territorial and protective of their positions.**

This political spirit begins to operate within the Body because members do the opposite of what Barnabas did and become territorial and protective of their positions—this is evidence of the leaven of Herod at work. Members of the Body seeking position and authority—bestowing upon themselves titles and honors—are not representing true apostolic government. If the government of God's Kingdom is to advance, we must release the wisdom of God—the wisdom of the cross—laying down our lives and preferring one another in love. *"Let nothing be done through selfish ambition or conceit, but in lowliness of mind let each esteem others better than himself"* (Phil. 2:3).

Just before divine government comes, you will see the political spirit rear its head and try to establish its own form of corrupt government again. It will begin with the seeds of envy in the hearts of men and women; envy will cause them to come against the very people that God is raising up to lead and protect them. The purpose for this is to prevent true and genuine apostolic government from being established for the release of God's Kingdom in the earth. If we are to learn to live under the rule of the government of God's Kingdom, we must learn to let love rule in our hearts. We must learn to heed the still, small voice of God's Spirit within our spirits saying, *"...Love does not envy..."* (1 Cor. 13:4).

Prepare the Way of the Lord

As John the Baptist went before Jesus declaring, *"Prepare the way of the Lord; make His paths straight"* (Mark 1:3), many people have end-time assignments that must be accomplished before Christ returns. These assignments will be about establishing God's divine order—an order that begins in the heart. Each believer must *"prepare the way for the Lord's coming"* by making *"clear the road for Him"* (NLT) in how they order their hearts and their lives.

Unlike those who *"...heard the voice of one crying in the wilderness"* (Mark 1:3), we have the voice of the Holy Spirit speaking directly to our hearts. We can *"[fix] our eyes on Jesus, the author and perfecter of [our] faith"* (Heb. 12:2 NASB). We can look to Christ as an example of how to defeat the political spirit that is opposing the Kingdom of God being released in and through us. He showed us how to walk in grace, truth, humility, meekness, and complete trust in the Father. He patiently allowed the wisdom of God to work on His behalf in order to take the wise in their own craftiness. In the process, He went to the cross. He allowed the love of God to rule and govern Him. *"By this we know love, because He laid down His life for us. And we also ought to lay down our lives for the brethren"* (1 John 3:16). And in what looked like defeat to His enemies, He won the ultimate victory.

This is how you differentiate between the rule of true and false government: one is self-sacrificing and promotes the interests of all while the other is self-seeking and promotes the interests of a select few. The only force strong enough to repel the deceptive cunning of the political spirit—and the only path to victory—is the way of righteousness, a righteousness that works by faith and a faith that works by love. *"For we through the Spirit eagerly wait for the hope of righteousness by faith. ...faith working through love"* (Gal. 5:5-6). The whole-hearted love and fear of God will cause you to walk in His ways. It will give you the wisdom and strength that you need to stand strong against the forces of evil. That is why God required Israel *"to fear the Lord your God, to walk in all His ways and to love Him, to serve the Lord your God with all your heart and with all your soul"* (Deut. 10:12). He was establishing His divine order for their protection.

When an individual is walking with God, his life will bring victory and blessing to many. But when the government of God is in place, countless multitudes will be blessed.

When one individual is walking with God, his life will bring victory and blessing to many. But when the government of God is in place, countless multitudes will be blessed. As with any government, however, there must be the backing of a justice system and military power. What happens when you betray the government by committing high treason? You are either exiled or executed. We who are under the government of God are not called to commit treason. We must align ourselves with the government of God's Kingdom according to divine order.

Those who are called to leadership have a responsibility to uphold true government. Leadership is about making choices through the wisdom of God and about having a hearing heart so that you can make righteous judgments—it is about securing the borders of His Kingdom by not allowing the political spirit to infiltrate the Church. That is true homeland security.

In Isaiah 42:16, God makes this promise: *"...I will lead them in paths they have not known. I will make darkness light before them, and crooked places straight. These things I will do for them, and not forsake them."* In Isaiah 35:8, Isaiah prophesies, *"A great road will go through that once deserted land. It will be named the Highway of Holiness. Evil-minded people will never travel on it. It will be only for those who walk in God's ways..."* (NLT).

The age of God's government is at hand. Hear what the Spirit of God is saying. Purify your heart. Cleanse your conscience. We must repent, forgive, and walk in love with all people, *"...lest Satan should take advantage of us; for we are not ignorant of his devices"* (2 Cor. 2:11).

This is truly an exciting time to be alive—it is a time filled with great opportunities and great dangers. As the people of God, we must discern His will and His wisdom, we must align ourselves with His plumb line and establish His purposes upon the earth as never before. It is time for His glory to shine in His temple once more. Prepare yourself and prepare the way of the Lord. He is coming. Now is the time to get ready to usher in His glory.

Meditation Points

- When you look into God's Word, what is He telling you to change? How is He asking you to align with His plumb line? What are the changes that need to come so that the government of His Kingdom can be established in your midst?

- How are you rightly dividing between what is coming out of your spirit from God and what is coming out of your soul from experience? Are you letting God's Word guide you in this, or is some other motivation obscuring God's will and assignment for your life?

- There is a great difference between the fear of the Lord and the fear of failure or hurt. Check to be sure that you are fearless when it comes to what you do and that you are walking in holy fear when it comes to who you are.

- Are you ready to conquer the political spirit in your world and to make way for divine government to flow in your sphere of influence?

Endnotes

1. "The Strongman of Zimbabwe," *The Week Daily*, June 28, 2008.

2. *Ibid.*

Ministry Contact Information

COVENANT OF LIFE MINISTRIES
COVENANT OF LIFE MEDIA INC.
PO BOX 27055
LETHBRIDGE, AB T1K 6Z8

E-MAIL: INFO@COVENANTOFLIFE.ORG

WEBSITE: WWW.COVENANTOFLIFE.ORG

PHONE: 1-877-220-3030
OUTSIDE NORTH AMERICA PHONE: 403-329-3038

Ministry Resources

THE PLUMBLINE
(AVAILABLE ON CD & DVD)
THIS PRODUCT ADDRESSES VARIOUS
QUESTIONS THAT WE ASK OURSELVES:

WHAT IS THE 'PLUMBLINE'?
HOW CAN I ALIGN MYSELF TO HEAVEN'S PLUMBLINE?
IS THERE A LARGER REASON WHY
MY PRAYERS ARE UNANSWERED?
IS MY LIFE BUILT ACCORDING TO THE PLUMBLINE?
GOD: PHARAOH OR FATHER?
HOW DO YOU SEE GOD? DO YOU SEE HIM
AS A LOVING FATHER OR A TASKMASTER?

IN ADDITION TO UNDERSTANDING
GOD'S TRUE NATURE, THIS DYNAMIC
MESSAGE OF HOPE WILL ALSO HELP
YOU DISCERN YOUR IDENTITY, PASSION,
AND PURPOSE.

LIFESTYLE EVANGELISM

(6 DISC CD & DVD SET)

IN THIS POWERFUL TRAINING SCHOOL YOU WILL UNDERSTAND:
HOW TO SHARE YOUR FAITH?
HOW TO REACH OUT TO PEOPLE
WITH A DIFFERENT BELIEF SYSTEM?

SPECIAL QUESTION & ANSWER SESSIONS.

To order, visit our Website:
www.covenantoflife.org.

Additional copies of this book and other
book titles from DESTINY IMAGE are
available at your local bookstore.

Call toll-free: 1-800-722-6774.

Send a request for a catalog to:

Destiny Image₍₎ Publishers, Inc.
P.O. Box 310
Shippensburg, PA 17257-0310

*"Speaking to the Purposes of God for This
Generation and for the Generations to Come."*

**For a complete list of our titles,
visit us at www.destinyimage.com.**

1 TIM 2.5
1 COR 3:11
JN 14:6
ACT 4:12